delicious. MAGAZINE

BAKING

HarperCollins*Publishers*
77–85 Fulham Palace Road,
Hammersmith, London W6 8JB
www.harpercollins.co.uk

First published by HarperCollins*Publishers* 2009

10 9 8 7 6 5 4 3 2 1

© Seven Publishing Group Ltd 2009

A catalogue record of this book is available from the British Library

ISBN-13   978-0-00-732838-3

Printed and bound in Hong Kong by Printing Express Limited

delicious. MAGAZINE
BAKING

Edited by Mitzie Wilson

Magazine Editor
Matthew Drennan

HarperCollins*Publishers*

contents

introduction   6

conversion tables   8

small bakes   10

classic cakes   44

chocolate   86

biscuits   104

bread and savoury baking   120

seasonal baking   150

icings and extras   182

index and acknowledgements   188

introduction

The idea of baking being a skill passed down from parent to child is lovely notion, but of course it's not always the case these days. In fact, as a nation we have all but forgotten how to bake a loaf of bread or make a simple Victoria sponge cake sandwiched with jam and cream and dusted with icing sugar. Home economics went out of the school window and shop-bought became the modern way.

The truth is, though, baking is not a skill we need to be scared of. While many savoury recipes can be interpreted to suit individual tastes, successful baking relies on one undisputable rule: stick to the recipe. Follow it to the letter and you won't go wrong. And you can't beat that home-baked taste; a cake made with fresh, good-quality ingredients is a world away from a shop-bought version. But the pleasure doesn't stop there; an afternoon spent in a warm kitchen making your own bread rolls, biscuits or chocolate brownies is a rewarding undertaking that's second to none.

In this book you'll find all the classics that are essential to any kitchen armoury, such as Coffee and walnut cake, meringues, fresh white bread or chocolate chip cookies, alongside new inventive bakes such as Gooseberry streusel cake with elderflower syrup, courgette muffins, chocolate beetroot cake and basil and goat's cheese cornbread.

At delicious. magazine all the recipes are tested in our kitchen until we are satisfied that they will read, cook and taste to the highest standards, every time.

Matthew Drennan
delicious. Magazine Editor

Conversion tables

All the recipes in this book list only metric measurements
(also used by Australian cooks). The conversions listed here
are approximate for imperial measurements (also used by
American cooks).

Oven temperatures

°C	Fan°C	°F	Gas	Description
110	90	225	¼	Very cool
120	100	250	½	Very cool
140	120	275	1	Cool
150	130	300	2	Cool
160	140	325	3	Warm
180	160	350	4	Moderate
190	170	375	5	Moderately hot
200	180	400	6	Fairly hot
220	200	425	7	Hot
230	210	450	8	Very hot
240	220	475	9	Very hot

Weights for dry ingredients

Metric	Imperial	Metric	Imperial
7g	¼oz	425g	15oz
15g	½oz	450g	1lb
20g	¾oz	500g	1lb 2oz
25g	1oz	550g	1¼lb
40g	1½oz	600g	1lb 5oz
50g	2oz	650g	1lb 7oz
60g	2½oz	675g	1½lb
75g	3oz	700g	1lb 9oz
100g	3½oz	750g	1lb 11oz
125g	4oz	800g	1¾lb
140g	4½oz	900g	2lb
150g	5oz	1kg	2¼lb
165g	5½oz	1.1kg	2½lb
175g	6oz	1.25kg	2¾lb
200g	7oz	1.35kg	3lb
225g	8oz	1.5kg	3lb 6oz
250g	9oz	1.8kg	4lb
275g	10oz	2kg	4½lb
300g	11oz	2.25kg	5lb
350g	12oz	2.5kg	5½lb
375g	13oz	2.75kg	6lb
400g	14oz	3kg	6¾lb

Liquid measures

Metric	Imperial	Aus	US
25ml	1fl oz		
50ml	2fl oz	¼ cup	¼ cup
75ml	3fl oz		
100ml	3½fl oz		
120ml	4fl oz	½ cup	½ cup
150ml	5fl oz		
175ml	6 fl oz	¾ cup	¾ cup
200ml	7fl oz		
250ml	8fl oz	1 cup	1 cup
300ml	10fl oz/½ pint	½ pint	1¼ cups
350ml	12fl oz		
400ml	14fl oz		
450ml	15fl oz	2 cups	2 cups/1 pint
600ml	1 pint	1 pint	2½ cups
750ml	1¼ pints		
900ml	1½ pints		
1 litre	1¾ pints	1¾ pints	1 quart
1.2 litres	2 pints		
1.4 litres	2½ pints		
1.5 litres	2¾ pints		
1.7 litres	3 pints		
2 litres	3½ pints		
3 litres	5¼ pints		

UK–Australian tablespoon conversions

1 x UK or Australian teaspoon is 5ml

1 x UK tablespoon is 3 teaspoons/15ml

1 Australian tablespoon is 4 teaspoons/20ml

small bakes

Chocolate cranberry muffins

Simple, light and very more-ish, these are perfect either for breakfast, with coffee or as part of afternoon tea.

MAKES 8 MUFFINS
TAKES 15 MINUTES, 22–25 MINUTES BAKING, PLUS COOLING

250g self-raising flour
½ tsp baking powder
½ tsp bicarbonate of soda
115g golden caster sugar
75g dried sweetened cranberries
100g plain chocolate (at least 50% cocoa solids), chopped
About 125ml milk
75ml sunflower oil
1 medium egg

1. Preheat the oven to 180°C/fan 160°C/ gas 4. Line a 12-hole muffin tin with 8 paper muffin cases.

2. Sift the flour, baking powder and bicarbonate of soda into a large bowl. Add the sugar and stir in the cranberries and chocolate.

3. In a small bowl, combine the milk, oil and egg, and whisk to blend well. Add to the dry ingredients and stir briefly until just combined. Don't overmix – the mixture should be thick and sticky. Stir in a splash of milk if it looks too dry.

4. Spoon into the muffin cases. Bake in the oven for 22–25 minutes, until golden, risen and firm, but springy. Remove and cool in the tin for 5 minutes, then transfer to a wire cooling rack. Serve warm.

Variation Make these muffins with any dried fruits such as raisins, cherries, strawberries or chopped apricots. You could add nuts instead of chocolate and a little ground mixed spice too.

Coconut slice

This traditional favourite tastes as great as ever. Bake up a batch to serve at a party – or keep in an airtight tin to enjoy whenever your sweet tooth strikes.

MAKES 21 SQUARES
TAKES 20 MINUTES, 20 MINUTES BAKING, PLUS COOLING

7 tbsp raspberry jam
3 egg whites
100g caster sugar
150g desiccated coconut
Toasted coconut flakes
  (optional)

For the pastry base
100g butter, plus extra for
  greasing
200g self-raising flour
50g caster sugar
2 egg yolks

1. Preheat the oven to 180°C/fan 160°C/gas 4. Grease a deep non-stick baking tin (about 17.5cm x 27cm x 4cm deep).

2. First make the pastry base. In a large bowl, rub the butter into the flour, then stir in the sugar. Mix in the egg yolks and 2 tablespoons cold water to form a moist dough. Press evenly into the base of the tin, then spread the jam on top.

3. In a clean bowl, whisk the egg whites to soft peaks. Using a large metal spoon, fold in the sugar and coconut. Spread over the jam, then scatter with the coconut flakes, if using. Bake for 20 minutes, or until the topping is golden. Cool in the tin, then cut into 21 squares to serve.

Lime and coconut slice

Give yourself a treat with these simple-to-make lime and coconut fancies.

MAKES 12 SLICES

TAKES 20 MINUTES, 40–45 MINUTES
BAKING, PLUS CHILLING AND COOLING

**200g unsalted butter, softened,
  plus extra for greasing**
250g plain flour
30g icing sugar
1 egg, lightly beaten

For the lime and coconut topping
6 eggs
375g caster sugar
25g plain flour
25g cornflour
**Finely grated zest and
  juice of 3 limes**
75g fresh coconut, shaved

1. Grease and base-line a 23cm-square baking tin. Put the butter, flour, icing sugar and egg in a food processor, and whiz to a soft dough. Press well into the tin, making sure it goes into the corners, and chill for 30 minutes.

2. Preheat the oven to 180°C/fan 160°C/gas 4. Bake the pastry base for 20–25 minutes until pale golden.

3. Meanwhile, make the topping. Whisk the eggs and add the sugar, flours, lime zest and juice, then whisk until pale and smooth. Pour on to the slice base and sprinkle over the coconut shavings. Don't worry if it seems thin; some mixture will go down the side of the pastry but it will set on cooking. Bake for 20–25 minutes, until set and lightly golden. Cool in the tin, then cut into squares and lift out one by one.

Power bars

These bars are packed with seeds and nuts for a tasty vitamin-powered snack.

MAKES 12–14 BARS
TAKES 15 MINUTES, 30 MINUTES BAKING, PLUS COOLING

175g butter, plus extra for greasing
175g golden syrup
250g light muscovado sugar
350g rolled oats
50g pumpkin seeds
50g golden linseed
50g hemp seeds
50g flaked almonds
50g ground almonds
75g dried cranberries
75g raisins

1. Preheat the oven to 190°C/fan 170°C/gas 5. Grease and line a shallow 23cm-square baking tin with baking paper.

2. Melt the butter, syrup and sugar in a pan over a low heat. Mix the remaining ingredients in a bowl. Pour over the syrup mix and combine well. Spread into the tin and press down with damp hands. Bake for 30 minutes, or until just golden brown on top.

3. Remove from the oven and cool for 10 minutes. Cut into bars in the tin. Cool completely before turning out whole and cutting again with a sharp knife.

Low-sugar low-fat flapjacks

We've used puréed dates instead of sugar to make these moist flapjacks. They're still rich, but a little less naughty than usual.

MAKES 12–14 FLAPJACKS
TAKES 20 MINUTES, 20–25 MINUTES
BAKING, PLUS COOLING

150g reduced-fat butter, plus extra for greasing
150g ready-to-eat soft stoned dates
3 tbsp apple juice
30g toasted whole hazelnuts, finely chopped
100g ready-to-eat dried apricots, finely chopped
225g porridge oats

1. Preheat the oven to 190°C/fan 170°C/gas 5. Grease and line a shallow 17.5cm-square baking tin with baking paper.

2. Put the dates and apple juice in a food processor, and whiz until smooth. Melt the butter in a large pan over a low heat. Add the date purée and all the other ingredients. Stir well, then press into the tin with damp hands. Bake for 20–25 minutes, or until just golden.

3. Remove from the oven and cool for 10 minutes. Cut into squares in the tin. Cool completely before turning out whole and cutting again with a sharp knife to separate.

Gooseberry streusel cake with elderflower syrup

Make the most of gooseberries with this amazing pudding that ~~... elderflower.~~

SERVES 10

TAKES ABOUT 30 MINUTES, ABOUT
1 HOUR BAKING, PLUS COOLING

600g fresh or frozen red
  or green gooseberries,
  stalks removed
2 tbsp elderflower cordial
300g caster sugar
400g plain flour
200g ground almonds
400g unsalted butter,
  chilled and cubed
75g flaked almonds
75g flaked coconut
Clotted cream, to serve

1. Preheat the oven to 190°C/fan 170°C/gas 5. Place the gooseberries, cordial, 100g of the caster sugar and 100ml water in a large saucepan over a gentle heat. Cook the fresh gooseberries for 4–5 minutes (frozen gooseberries for 8–9 minutes), stirring occasionally, until they have wilted and released their juices. Strain, reserving the juices, and set both aside to cool.

2. Meanwhile, put the flour, ground almonds and remaining caster sugar in a food processor. Add the butter and whiz until the mixture is like coarse breadcrumbs. Transfer half to a bowl, toss with the flaked almonds and coconut, and set aside.

3. Line a 30cm x 23cm baking tin with baking paper. Whiz the remaining crumbs again until they form a smooth dough. Using your fingers, press the dough into the base of the baking tin in an even layer, leaving a rim all around. Prick the base and bake for 15 minutes, until pale golden.

4. Spoon the strained gooseberries over the base, scatter the crumb, almond and coconut mixture on top, and bake for 45–50 minutes, until golden and crisp and the juices are bubbling. Cool slightly in the tin, then remove carefully using the paper.

5. Simmer the reserved gooseberry juices in a small pan for a few minutes until reduced and syrupy. Cool completely.

6. Cut the cake into wedges, drizzle with the syrup and serve with a dollop of clotted cream.

Apple, pecan and raisin muffins

This delicious recipe for healthy Golden Delicious muffins comes from the book *A Basket of Apples,* by British painter and cook Val Archer. These are great for breakfast and terrific served hot with apple curd.

MAKES 12 MUFFINS

TAKES 20 MINUTES, 25–30 MINUTES BAKING, PLUS COOLING

75g butter, melted, plus extra
  for greasing
300ml skimmed milk
125g oat bran
2 eggs
75g light muscovado sugar
½ tsp vanilla extract
60g wholemeal flour
125g self-raising flour
2 tsp baking powder
2 Golden Delicious apples,
  peeled, cored and chopped
2 tbsp raisins soaked in
  2 tbsp rum or orange juice
25g pecan nuts, toasted and
  chopped

1. Preheat the oven to 190°C/fan 170°C/gas 5. Grease a 12-hole muffin tin with a little butter. Put the milk and oat bran in a bowl, and set aside.

2. In a small bowl, beat together the eggs, butter, sugar and vanilla.

3. In a larger bowl, sift together the flours, ½ teaspoon salt and baking powder, and stir in the apple.

4. Add the bran mix into the egg mixture, then briefly stir this into the flour and apple. Divide the mixture into two. Briefly stir the raisins and their soaking mixture into one half, and the pecans into the other.

5. Put a heaped dessertspoonful of each mixture into the muffin holes so you get 6 of each flavour. Bake in the oven for 25–30 minutes, or until risen and golden. Cool in the tin for 10 minutes, then turn out on to a wire rack. Serve the muffins warm or at room temperature.

Variation Instead of the apple, add 2 small ripe bananas, chopped, and instead of the raisins use 50g chopped plain chocolate.

Courgette muffins or cake

If you think carrot cake sounds a bit strange, why not confound your friends with this courgette version. Don't knock these moreish munchies until you've tried them.

SERVES **12**

TAKES **20** MINUTES, **25–30** MINUTES BAKING FOR THE MUFFINS AND **45–50** MINUTES FOR THE CAKE, PLUS COOLING

250g courgettes, roughly grated

100g sultanas

4 tbsp fresh orange juice

2 tbsp clear honey

3 large free-range eggs

175ml sunflower oil

200g light muscovado sugar

225g self-raising flour

½ tsp baking powder

½ tsp bicarbonate of soda

60g almonds, toasted and chopped

Grated zest of 2 limes, plus extra to decorate

1 quantity cream cheese icing (see page 183)

Juice of 2 limes

Almonds, toasted and finely chopped, to decorate

1. Preheat the oven to 180°C/fan 160°C/gas 4. Line a 12-hole muffin tin with muffin cases (or, to make 1 big cake, grease and line a 23cm-round loose-bottomed cake tin).

2. Squeeze the grated courgettes by hand to drain excess moisture. Pat dry with kitchen paper.

3. Put the sultanas in a saucepan with the orange juice and honey. Bring to a boil and simmer for 4 minutes until the sultanas are plump and the liquid is absorbed, being careful not to let it burn.

4. Put the eggs, sunflower oil and sugar in a large bowl and whisk with an electric whisk for about 3 minutes, until creamy. Sift over the flour, baking powder and bicarbonate of soda. Fold in with the almonds, the grated courgettes, the drained sultanas and the lime zest.

5. Spoon into the muffin cases or tin and bake the muffins for 25–30 minutes or the cake for 45–50 minutes or until a skewer inserted into the centre comes out clean.

6. Leave the muffins or cake to cool in their tins, then transfer to a wire rack to cool completely. Beat the cream cheese icing with the lime juice until smooth and creamy, adding more icing sugar to taste, if needed.

7. Spread the icing over the muffins or the cake. Sprinkle with the finely chopped almonds and more lime zest.

Spiced pumpkin muffins with cream cheese icing

Don't throw away the pumpkin flesh when you make your Halloween lantern – use it to rustle up these very moist and more-ish muffins.

MAKES 12

TAKES 25 MINUTES, 15–20 MINUTES BAKING, PLUS COOLING

225g self-raising flour
1 tsp bicarbonate of soda
1 tsp ground ginger
150ml sunflower oil
150ml soured cream
225g caster sugar
2 large eggs
125g piece pumpkin or butternut squash, coarsely grated
75g walnut pieces, chopped
1 quantity cream cheese icing (see page 183)
Pinch of ground cinnamon

For the decoration
Tangerine food colouring
150g marzipan
Tube of black writing icing

1. Preheat the oven to 200°C/fan 180°C/gas 6. Line a 12-hole muffin tin with paper cases.

2. Put the flour, bicarbonate of soda and ground ginger in a bowl. Pour the oil into a jug and add the soured cream, sugar and eggs, then beat with a fork until well blended. Pour the wet ingredients into the dry, then add the pumpkin and walnuts, and stir well.

3. Spoon into the paper cases and bake for 15–20 minutes, until well risen and firm. Leave to cool.

4. Beat the cream cheese icing with the cinnamon until smooth. Spread the icing over the tops of the cooled muffins.

5. For the decorations, add a few drops of the food colouring to the marzipan and knead until you have a deep pumpkin colour. Break off walnut-sized pieces of the coloured marzipan and roll into balls. Mark lines for a pumpkin look using the back of a knife. Decorate with the black icing and position on top of the muffins.

Chocolate toffee crispy cakes

These cakes are an absolute classic, and a must for any trainee cook.

MAKES ABOUT 24 CAKES
TAKES 15 MINUTES, PLUS AT LEAST 1 HOUR SETTING

100g toffees
100g unsalted butter
100g marshmallows
1 tbsp cocoa powder
100g Rice Krispies

1. Put 24 paper or foil cake cases into 2 x 12-hole fairy-cake tins. If you don't have these tins, just rest the cases on a large platter.

2. Put the toffees, butter and marshmallows in a pan. Heat very gently, stirring occasionally with a wooden spoon, until everything has melted and the mixture is smooth – this will only take 3 minutes. Add the cocoa powder and mix together.

3. Take the pan off the heat. Carefully stir in the cereal – the mix will be very hot. Using 2 spoons, spoon the mixture into the paper cases. Leave in a cool place for at least 1 hour to set. Keep in an airtight container in a cool place for up to 3 days.

Variation For plain crispy cakes, just leave out the cocoa powder. You can also use cornflakes instead of Rice Krispies, if you prefer.

Raspberry tarts with iced frangipane

Try these dainty little cherry bakewells for afternoon tea.

MAKES 12 TARTS
TAKES 40 MINUTES, 40–45 MINUTES
BAKING, PLUS CHILLING AND COOLING

1 quantity rich shortcrust
  pastry (see page 184)
24 tsp raspberry jam

For the topping
65g softened butter, plus extra
  for greasing
65g caster sugar
1 large free-range egg
2 tsp rum
1 tbsp plain flour
65g ground almonds
175g icing sugar
1½ tbsp fresh lemon juice
12 dried cranberries,
  to decorate

1. Preheat the oven to 200°C/fan 180°C/gas 6. Thinly roll out the pastry on a floured surface. Press out 12 circles with an 8cm cutter and use to line a greased 12-hole mince pie or bun tin. Spoon 2 teaspoons raspberry jam into each pastry case.

2. In a bowl, cream the butter with the caster sugar until light and fluffy. Gradually add the egg and rum. Fold in the plain flour and ground almonds.

3. Spoon on to the pies and bake for about 25–30 minutes, until golden. Cool on a wire rack.

4. Mix the icing sugar with lemon juice, then spoon over the pies. Allow the icing to set and decorate each with a dried cranberry.

Streusel

A German tray bake with mincemeat that makes a great
alternative at Christmas to traditional mince pies.

SERVES 6–8
TAKES 30 MINUTES, 30–35 MINUTES
BAKING, PLUS CHILLING AND COOLING

Flour, for dusting
2 quantities rich shortcrust
  pastry (see page 184)
700g jar mincemeat (or make
  your own, see page 186)

For the topping
100g plain flour
50g ground almonds
50g caster sugar
135g cold unsalted butter,
  cubed
25g dried cranberries
25g flaked almonds
Icing sugar, to dust

1 Preheat the oven to 200°C/fan 180°C/gas 6.
Thinly roll out the pastry on a floured surface and
use to line the base and sides of a 20cm x 27cm
rectangular, loose-bottomed fluted tart tin – you
may not need all the pastry.

2. Prick the base with a fork and fill with baking
paper and beans. Blind bake for 10 minutes, then
remove the paper and beans, and return to the
oven for 5 minutes.

3. Spread the mincemeat over the pastry base.

4. In a bowl, mix together the plain flour, ground
almonds and caster sugar. Rub in the butter,
until it becomes crumb-like. Stir in the dried
cranberries and flaked almonds. Scatter the
mixture over the mincemeat.

5. Bake for 15–20 minutes, until golden. Cool and
dust with icing sugar.

Date crumb cake

This moist crumbly cake is great for afternoon tea or packed lunches.

MAKES 21 SQUARES
TAKES 20 MINUTES, 20–25 MINUTES
BAKING, PLUS COOLING

125g butter, plus extra for
  greasing
250g dried ready-to-eat dates,
  chopped
250g self-raising flour
250g dark muscovado sugar,
  sifted
2 tbsp oats
½ tsp ground cinnamon
1 egg, lightly beaten

1. Preheat the oven to 180°C/fan 160°C/ gas 4. Grease a deep non-stick baking tin (about 17.5cm x 27cm x 4cm).

2. Pour 6 tablespoons boiling water over the dates. Leave for 5 minutes to soften, then whiz to a rough paste in a food processor.

3. Sift the flour and sugar into a large bowl, add the butter and rub in until just crumb-like. Tip half the mixture into another bowl and stir in the oats. Rub the remaining mixture until the crumbs are very fine, then stir in the cinnamon and egg to get a moist dough. Press this evenly into the base of the tin.

4. Spread the date mixture over the dough base, then sprinkle over the oaty crumb mixture, pressing down lightly. Bake for 20–25 minutes, until the topping is golden. Cool in the tin and cut into 21 squares to serve.

Variation Use dried apricots instead of dates, if liked.

Black cherry and pistachio cereal bars

A deliciously chewy and very quick breakfast or coffee-time bar.

MAKES 15 BARS
TAKES 10 MINUTES, PLUS
25–30 MINUTES BAKING

150g granola
50g shelled pistachio nuts
100g dried black cherries
200ml ready-made apple sauce
50g ground almonds

1. Preheat the oven to 160°C/fan 140°C/gas 3. Base-line a 23cm-square tin with baking paper. Mix the granola, pistachios and cherries with the apple sauce and ground almonds, and press into the tin.

2. Bake for 25–30 minutes, until pale golden. Cool completely in the tin, turn out and cut into 15 bars. These will keep in an airtight container for up to 2 days.

Chocolate meringues

These mega meringues are a real indulgence and as good as those you see in expensive bakeries!

MAKES 6 LARGE MERINGUES
TAKES 15 MINUTES, 1 HOUR BAKING, PLUS DRYING AND COOLING

4 large egg whites
225g white caster sugar
15g sieved cocoa powder
25g chopped toasted hazelnuts (optional)
25g chopped pistachio nuts (optional)

1. Preheat the oven to 140°C/fan 120°C/gas 1, and line a baking sheet with non-stick baking paper.

2. Whisk the egg whites until soft well-defined peaks form (hold the bowl upside down – the whites should stay in the bowl). Overshooting by more whisking will 'burst the bubbles' and release all that precious air you have incorporated into the whites.

3. Whisk in about half the caster sugar, a little at a time until you get glossy stiff peaks. Slowly fold in the remaining sugar with a large, very clean metal spoon, taking care not to knock out any air, until you have a stiff yet soft meringue mixture. Towards the end of this stage, barely fold in the cocoa powder to obtain a streaky effect with pockets of powdery cocoa.

4. Put a blob of meringue on the underside of the baking paper lining the baking tray to hold it in place. Using 2 large metal spoons, drop piles of meringue on to the paper, making a shape as swirly or craggy as you like. Space them well apart.?Scatter with the hazelnuts and pistachios, if using.

5. Bake in the oven for 1 hour. Turn off the oven and leave the meringues in there for at least 4 hours, or overnight, to dry out. Store the meringues in an airtight container and keep for up to 4 days.

Variation Omit the cocoa and nuts for plain meringues, or add chopped dried strawberries or cherries and a little pink food colouring for glorious red berry ones.

Mocha meringues

Give your coffee-loving friends and any chocoholics a treat with these mocha meringues.

MAKES 30 MERINGUES
TAKES 30 MINUTES, 45 MINUTES
BAKING, PLUS COOLING AND SETTING

3 large organic egg whites
175g white caster sugar
½ tsp vanilla extract
15g sifted cocoa powder
1 tbsp espresso coffee powder
150g plain chocolate
Whipped cream, to serve

1. Preheat the oven to 140°C/fan 120°C/gas 1. In a large, grease-free mixing bowl, whisk the egg whites to soft peaks. While continuously whisking, slowly add the caster sugar – 1 tablespoon at a time – until you have a stiff, glossy meringue mixture. Whisk in the vanilla extract, cocoa powder and 2 teaspoons espresso coffee powder until combined.

2. Spoon into a piping bag with a 1cm plain nozzle. Pipe 60 small blobs on to 2 lined baking sheets. Bake for 45 minutes, then cool on a wire rack.

3. Melt the plain chocolate with the remaining coffee powder in a bowl set over a pan of simmering water. Cool. Use this spread to sandwich 2 meringue bases together. When set, serve with cream.

classic cakes

Victoria sponge cake

We couldn't have a baking book without including our classic
Victoria sponge recipe.

SERVES 8
TAKES 20 MINUTES, 25–30 MINUTES
BAKING, PLUS COOLING

225g butter, softened,
  plus extra for greasing
225g golden caster sugar
4 medium eggs, beaten
225g self-raising flour
4 tbsp raspberry jam
Whipped cream (optional)
Icing sugar, to dust

1. Preheat the oven to 180°C/fan 160°C/gas 4.
Grease and base-line 2 x 20cm-round sponge tins
with baking paper.

2. Put the butter and sugar into a mixing bowl and
beat with a wooden spoon or electric mixer until
light, fluffy and pale cream coloured. Gradually add
the eggs, beating well after each addition to get a
smooth emulsion. If the mixture starts to curdle,
add a spoonful of the flour. Sift the flour into the
bowl and fold it in with a large metal spoon until
the mixture is smooth.

3. Divide the mixture equally between the
2 tins and smooth it flat. Bake in the oven for
25–30 minutes until golden and firm but springy to
the touch. Turn the layers out on to a cooling rack.
When they have cooled, peel off the paper and
sandwich the cakes together with jam. (You could
also add a layer of whipped cream, if you like.)
Dust with icing sugar just before serving.

Variation To make butterfly cakes: divide the
mixture among 12 cupcake cases and bake for
15–20 minutes until golden brown and just firm to
the touch. Cool, then cut off the domed tops and
slice in half to make wings. Top each cake with
vanilla buttercream (see page 182) and the wings.

Mini Victoria sponge cakes

Try this mini variation on a conventional Victoria sponge.

MAKES 4 CAKES TO SERVE 8
TAKES 50 MINUTES, ABOUT
20 MINUTES BAKING, PLUS COOLING

170g unsalted butter, softened,
   plus extra for greasing
170g caster sugar
3 medium eggs
1 tsp vanilla extract
170g self-raising flour
284ml carton whipping cream
Icing sugar, for dusting

For the strawberry jam
450g strawberries, hulled
500g preserving sugar
Juice of 1 lemon

1. First, make the jam. Put 2 saucers in the freezer. Put the strawberries, sugar and lemon juice in a preserving pan or wide, deep pan over a medium–low heat, stirring until the sugar has dissolved. Bring to the boil for 6 minutes. Remove from the heat. Put a spoonful on to a chilled saucer and push your finger through it – if it wrinkles, it's ready; if not, boil for another 2 minutes and repeat. Discard any surface scum and stand for 15 minutes.

2. Spoon into sterilised jars. Cool, cover with waxed discs and store in a cool place for up to 3 months.

3. Preheat the oven to 180°C/fan 160°C/gas 4. Grease and base-line 2 Yorkshire pudding tins with 4 x 8–9cm straight-sided holes, or 8 round plain cutters sat on 2 lined baking sheets.

4. Put the butter and sugar in a large bowl and, using an electric hand whisk, beat until fluffy. Lightly beat the eggs with the vanilla, then gradually beat into the creamed mixture, adding a little flour. Sift over the remaining flour and gently fold in until just combined.

5. Divide evenly among the holes or rings, smoothing the surface. Bake for 12 minutes, swap the tins around and bake for 10 minutes more or until risen and golden. Cool for 10 minutes in the tin, then turn out on to a wire rack and cool.

6. Lightly whip the cream to soft peaks. Spread on to 4 sponge bases, top with some of the jam and sandwich with the remaining sponge discs. Dust each with icing sugar to serve.

Dundee cake

A slice of this traditional Scottish fruit cake is perfect with a cup of tea. You could use the mixture for a Christmas cake, too.

SERVES 8–10
TAKES 30 MINUTES, SOAKING TIME,
1¼ HOURS BAKING, PLUS COOLING

120g currants
120g raisins
100g natural-coloured glacé
  cherries
60g mixed citrus peel, chopped
Grated zest of 1 orange
Grated zest of 1 lemon
2 tbsp whisky
170g unsalted butter, softened,
  plus extra for greasing
170g golden caster sugar
4 medium eggs
170g plain flour
1 tsp baking powder
1 tsp ground mixed spice
60g ground almonds
80g whole blanched almonds

1. Place the dried fruits, cherries, citrus peel and zests in a bowl with the whisky. Mix, cover, and set aside for 1 hour.

2. Preheat the oven to 150°C/fan 130°C/gas 2. Grease and line the base and sides of a deep 20cm-wide cake tin with baking paper.

3. Put the butter and sugar into a large bowl. Using an electric whisk, beat until light and fluffy. Beat in the eggs, one at a time, until well combined, adding a little flour to prevent curdling. Sift over the remaining flour, baking powder and spice, and mix. Using a wooden spoon, mix in the ground almonds and drained soaked dried fruits. Spoon into the cake tin, level the surface and decorate the top with whole almonds, pressing them slightly into the mixture.

4. Bake for 1¼ hours, but check after 30 minutes that it's not browning too much. If it is, cover the cake with a double sheet of baking paper. To test whether the cake is cooked, insert a skewer into the centre – if it comes out clean, the cake is ready. Cool completely in the tin.

5. Wrap the cake in greaseproof paper, then in foil, and store in an airtight tin. It will keep for up to 2 weeks.

Parkin

This dense, crumbly cake has been eaten around the fire on Bonfire Night in Yorkshire for centuries.

SERVES 12
TAKES 15 MINUTES, 45 MINUTES BAKING, PLUS COOLING

140g unsalted butter, plus
  extra for greasing and serving
100g dark muscovado sugar
4 tbsp black treacle
200g plain flour
1 tsp baking powder
¼ tsp bicarbonate of soda
2 tsp ground ginger
Good pinch of ground mace
Good pinch of ground cloves
150g medium oatmeal
150g glacé ginger, chopped
1 egg
100ml milk

1. Preheat the oven to 150°C/ fan 130°C/gas 2. Grease and base-line a deep 23cm-square cake tin with baking paper. Melt the butter, sugar and treacle in a pan over a low heat, stirring. Take off the heat and cool for 10 minutes.

2. Sift the flour, baking powder, bicarbonate of soda, ground spices and a pinch of salt in a bowl. Add the oatmeal and two-thirds of the glacé ginger.

3. In another bowl, beat the egg and milk, then add to the flour with the treacle mix. Mix well. Pour into the tin and sprinkle over the remaining ginger. Bake for 45 minutes, until just firm.

4. Stand the tin on a wire rack and cool for about 20 minutes. Turn out to cool completely. Serve slices spread with butter. It will keep in an airtight tin for up to 2 weeks, where it will become more moist.

Eccles cakes

These originated in the Lancashire town of Eccles (meaning church) apparently served after annual church services – known as 'Eccles Wakes' – in the Middle Ages. Divine served with Cheshire cheese.

MAKES 12 CAKES
TAKES 25 MINUTES, 15 MINUTES
BAKING, PLUS COOLING

Flour, for dusting
425g frozen ready-rolled
  puff pastry, thawed
3 tbsp milk
4 tbsp demerara sugar

For the filling
75g unsalted butter, plus extra
  for greasing
200g currants
75g chopped mixed peel
1½ tsp ground mixed spice
50g light muscovado sugar

1. Preheat the oven to 230°C/ fan 210°C/gas 8 and grease a baking sheet. Put all the ingredients for the filling into a small pan and heat gently until the sugar has dissolved and the butter has melted. Mix, then take off the heat and leave to cool.

2. Dust a work surface with flour and roll out the pastry thinly. Use an 11.5cm pastry cutter to cut out 12 rounds. Put a large teaspoonful of the filling in the centre of each round, then fold in and seal to enclose the mixture.

3. Turn the pastry rounds over and press gently with a rolling pin to flatten. Cut 3 slits in the top of each cake and place on the baking sheet. Brush with milk and sprinkle with demerara sugar. Bake for about 15 minutes, until golden (the currants will bulge through the pastry). Best eaten fresh and warm.

Richmond maids of honour

Believed to have originated at Hampton Court Palace under Henry VIII, these almond tarts were reportedly named after Anne Boleyn. Though she later became his second wife, Anne was once the maid of honour to Henry's first wife, Catherine of Aragon.

MAKES **10–12** TARTS
TAKES **15** MINUTES, **20–25** MINUTES
BAKING, PLUS COOLING

Flour, for dusting
375g pack chilled dessert pastry
75g unsalted butter, plus extra
   for greasing
110g curd cheese
1 egg
1 tbsp brandy
75g golden caster sugar
50g ground almonds
Finely grated zest of 1 lemon

1. Preheat the oven to 200°C/ fan 180°C/gas 6. Lightly dust a work surface with flour, then roll out the pastry to about the thickness of a pound coin. Cut out 10–12 x 10cm circles with a pastry cutter, and use to line 10–12 greased deep tartlet or bun tins.

2. In a bowl, beat the cheese and butter together until smooth, then beat in the egg and brandy, followed by the sugar, almonds and lemon zest. Spoon the mixture into the pastry cases to half-fill them.

3. Bake for 20–25 minutes until risen and golden. Remove the tarts from the oven and put on a wire rack to cool. They will sink a little when cooled. Keep for up to 2 days in an airtight container.

Variation Although it's not traditional, you could add a teaspoon of your favourite jam to the pastry base before you add the filling.

Vanilla sponge with crème pâtissière and gooseberry compote

This delightfully old-fashioned sponge recipe has a delicious sweet and tart combination of flavours and is a real taste of summer.

SERVES 8–10

TAKES 40 MINUTES, 20–25 MINUTES BAKING, PLUS COOLING

225g butter, softened,
  plus extra for greasing
225g caster sugar
4 large free-range eggs
225g self-raising flour
1 tsp vanilla extract
4 tbsp milk
Icing sugar, to dust

For the crème pâtissière
250ml full-fat milk
½ vanilla pod, split lengthways
  and seeds scraped
3 large free-range egg yolks
45g caster sugar
40g cornflour
142ml carton double cream
2 tbsp elderflower cordial

For the gooseberry compote
400g fresh or frozen and
  thawed gooseberries
50g caster sugar, plus extra
  to taste
2 tbsp elderflower cordial

1. Preheat the oven to 180°C/fan 160°C/gas 4. Butter and base-line 2 x 20cm-round cake tins with baking paper. Cream the butter and sugar until fluffy, then gradually mix in the eggs with a little of the flour. Fold in the remaining flour, vanilla and milk, until smooth. Divide between the tins, level, and bake for 20–25 minutes. Cool for 10 minutes, then turn out on to a wire rack and cool completely.

2. Meanwhile, make the crème pâtissière. Heat the milk, vanilla pod and seeds in a small pan, until simmering. Whisk the yolks, sugar and cornflour in a bowl. Slowly whisk in the hot milk and return to the pan. Cook, stirring, for 2 minutes, until very thick. Discard the pod, cover the surface with cling film and cool.

3. For the compote, put the gooseberries and sugar in a small pan over a medium heat. Cook for 10 minutes (13–14 minutes if frozen), stirring occasionally, until soft. Stir in the elderflower cordial – add more sugar if it's tart. Cool completely.

4. Whisk the cream and elderflower cordial to stiff peaks. Whisk in some crème pâtissière to loosen, then fold in the rest. Spread on to the flat side of 1 cake, then top with the gooseberry compote. Sandwich with the other cake, flat-side down, then dust with icing sugar to serve.

Apricot buttermilk cake

This fresh-tasting, light cake is bursting with the flavours of summer fruits, topped with contrasting crunchy almonds.

SERVES 12
TAKES 20 MINUTES, 40–45 MINUTES BAKING, PLUS COOLING

175g butter, very soft,
   plus extra for greasing
200g self-raising flour
150g ground almonds
200g golden caster sugar
150ml buttermilk
3 large free-range eggs, beaten
1 tsp vanilla extract
Finely grated zest of 1 lemon
6 ripe apricots, halved and
   stoned
2 tbsp mild runny honey
50g flaked almonds

For the honey cream
142ml carton double cream
150ml Greek-style yogurt
4 tbsp mild runny honey

1. Preheat the oven to 180°C/fan 160°C/ gas 4. Grease and base-line a 30cm x 23cm x 5cm deep baking tin with baking paper. Whiz together all the dry ingredients in a food processor. Add the butter, buttermilk, eggs, vanilla and lemon zest, and pulse until combined.

2. Pour the mixture into the tin, level and arrange the apricots on top, cut-side up. Drizzle with honey and sprinkle with the almonds. Bake for 40–45 minutes, then set aside to cool in the tin for 20 minutes.

3. Meanwhile, whip together the cream, yogurt and honey until thickened. Serve the cake with the honey cream.

Variation Instead of apricots, use either halved plums or canned, well-drained pineapple rings. You could even try rhubarb when it's in season.

Moist ginger cake

This sticky, spicy cake is great for elevenses, or for a snack while you're on the go. The rich taste of the ginger will leave your taste buds tingling.

SERVES 8

TAKES 15 MINUTES, 50–55 MINUTES BAKING, PLUS COOLING

100g unsalted butter,
    plus extra for greasing
100g dark muscovado sugar
75g golden syrup
100ml milk
1 large egg, beaten
150g plain flour
1 tsp bicarbonate of soda
2 tsp ground ginger
2 tsp ground cinnamon
75g ready-to-eat prunes,
    chopped
225g golden icing sugar
40g crystallised root ginger,
    sliced

1. Preheat the oven to 150°C/fan 130°C/gas 2. Grease and base-line a deep 20cm-round springform cake tin or use a cake liner, if you like.

2. Put the butter, sugar and syrup in a saucepan and gently melt, stirring all the time. Stir in the milk, then tip into a jug to cool. Stir in the egg.

3. Sift the flour, bicarbonate of soda and spices into a large bowl and make a well in the centre. Stir in the syrup mixture and the prunes. Pour into the tin and bake for 50–55 minutes, or until a skewer inserted into the centre comes out clean. Cool in the tin, then turn out on to a serving plate.

4. Sieve the icing sugar into a bowl and mix to a smooth consistency with 2–2½ tablespoons hot water. Pour over the cake and decorate with ginger. Let the icing set before slicing the cake.

Cranberry fruit loaf with cranberry sauce

This beautiful alternative to Christmas cake, adapted from Jane Grigson's *Fruit Book*, would make a great teatime treat over the holidays.

CUTS INTO 12 SLICES
TAKES 25 MINUTES, 55 MINUTES
BAKING, PLUS COOLING

3 tbsp hazelnut oil or melted
  butter, plus extra for greasing
500g plain flour, sifted
225g golden caster sugar
4 tsp baking powder
2 eggs, beaten
350ml whole milk
200g fresh (or frozen and
  thawed) cranberries, coarsely
  chopped
100g mixed dried fruit
100g skinned roasted hazelnuts,
  roughly chopped
Butter or cream cheese, to
  serve (optional)

For the cranberry sauce
200g fresh or frozen cranberries
100g caster sugar
Seeds from ½ vanilla pod or
  ¼ tsp vanilla extract
Juice of 4 small oranges

1. Preheat the oven to 180°C/fan 160°C/gas 4. Grease and base-line a deep 2-litre loaf tin. Sift the flour, sugar, baking powder and 1 teaspoon salt into a large bowl. Beat the eggs, milk and oil or butter in another bowl, then fold into the dry ingredients, followed by the fruit and nuts.

2. Spoon the mixture into the loaf tin and bake for 55 minutes, or until a skewer inserted into the middle comes out clean. Remove from the oven and leave to cool in the tin for 10 minutes, then turn out on to a wire rack to cool completely.

3. Meanwhile, make the sauce. Put the cranberries, sugar, vanilla and orange juice in a saucepan over a medium heat. Cook for 6–8 minutes, stirring occasionally, until the fruit breaks down and the mix looks jammy. Set aside to cool and thicken.

4. Serve the cake in slices with the cranberry sauce and some butter or cream cheese, if you wish.

Parsnip and fruit loaf with lemon drizzle

A fruit loaf made from parsnips? Whatever next! (Oh, did we mention how ruddy lovely it tastes?)

SERVES 10–12

TAKES 20 MINUTES, 50 MINUTES–
1 HOUR BAKING, PLUS COOLING

200g mixed dried fruit
4 tbsp fresh orange juice
2 tbsp honey
3 large free-range eggs
175ml sunflower oil
200g light muscovado sugar
225g self-raising flour
½ tsp baking powder
½ tsp bicarbonate of soda
1 tsp ground ginger
1 tsp ground mixed spice
Grated zest of 1 lemon
225g parsnips, grated

For the icing
250g natural yogurt
Juice of 1 lemon
50g icing sugar

1. Grease and line a 2-litre loaf tin (a traditional high-sided bread loaf tin) with non-stick baking paper. Preheat the oven to 180°C/fan 160°C/gas 4.

2. Place the mixed dried fruit in a saucepan with the orange juice and honey, and bring to the boil. Simmer for 2 minutes until the fruit is plump and the liquid has been absorbed.

3. Put the eggs, sunflower oil and sugar in a large bowl and whisk with an electric hand whisk for about 3 minutes until creamy. Sift over self-raising flour, baking powder, bicarbonate of soda, ground ginger, mixed spice and the grated lemon zest. Fold into the mix with the parsnips and the drained mixed fruit mixture. Spoon into the prepared tin and bake in the oven for 50 minutes–1 hour, or until a skewer inserted into the centre comes out clean.

4. For the icing, beat together the natural yogurt with the lemon juice and icing sugar. While the cake is still warm, drizzle the icing over it, then transfer the cake to a cooling rack to cool completely.

Ginger loaf cake

This flavoursome loaf is more of a tea bread than a sweet cake. And it's oh-so-simple to make.

MAKES 1 CAKE TO CUT INTO 12 SLICES
TAKES 20 MINUTES, 1¼ HOURS
BAKING, PLUS COOLING

125g unsalted butter, softened, plus extra for greasing
350g plain flour
1 tsp baking powder
1 tsp bicarbonate of soda
3–4 tsp ground ginger
8 globes preserved stem ginger in syrup, drained
100g light muscovado sugar
225g golden syrup
1 organic egg, beaten
75ml milk

1. Grease and base-line a 900g loaf tin (a traditional high-sided bread loaf tin) with non-stick baking paper. Preheat the oven to 160°C/fan 140°C/gas 3.

2. Sift together the flour, baking powder, bicarbonate of soda and ground ginger. Set aside. Chop 4 globes of the ginger and add to the flour mixture. Finely slice the remainder and set aside.

3. Melt the butter, sugar and golden syrup in a small pan. Set aside to cool slightly (this should take about 15 minutes).

4. Beat the egg and milk together. Stir the cooled syrup into the dry ingredients, followed by the egg and milk, and beat well. Spoon into the tin and arrange the remaining ginger overlapping on top. Bake for about 1¼ hours until just firm to the touch. Cool on a wire rack.

★ DELICIOUS. TIP This cake is at its best eaten within a day or two, or you can revive it in a warm oven for 5 minutes. Serve it warm or cold, in thick slices with lashings of butter.

Hazelnut meringue roulade

This is a luxurious afternoon treat, but it's easier to make than you might think.

SERVES 8
TAKES 20 MINUTES, PLUS
15 MINUTES BAKING

Butter, for greasing
3 large organic egg whites
175g white caster sugar
½ tsp white wine vinegar
1 tsp cornflour
40g toasted chopped hazelnuts,
  plus extra to decorate
284ml carton double cream
2 tbsp Nutella
Icing sugar, to dust

1. Grease and line a 22cm x 32cm Swiss-roll tin with baking paper, so it forms a collar. Preheat the oven to 190°C/fan 170°C/gas 5.

2. In a large, grease-free mixing bowl, whisk the egg whites to soft peaks. While continuously whisking, slowly add the caster sugar – 1 tablespoon at a time – until you have a stiff, glossy meringue mixture. Whisk in the wine vinegar and cornflour until combined. Fold in the hazelnuts and spread in the tin. Bake in the oven for 15 minutes.

3. Turn out on to baking paper. Whip the cream to soft peaks and fold in the Nutella. Spread over the cooled roulade and roll up, using the paper to keep it tight, but not rolling it into the roulade. Dust with icing sugar and scatter with more chopped hazelnuts.

Almond cake in spiced citrus syrup

Try this simple almond cake made with oranges and lemons
to give it a zesty citric kick.

SERVES 8

TAKES 45 MINUTES, 45 MINUTES
BAKING, PLUS COOLING

Butter, for greasing
6 medium eggs, separated
225g caster sugar, plus 1 tbsp
  extra
230g ground almonds
Finely grated zest of 2 oranges
Finely grated zest of 1 lemon

For the syrup
50g caster sugar
Juice of 1 orange
Juice of 1 large lemon
1 star anise
1 large cinnamon stick
2 cardamom pods, lightly
  crushed

For the orange fruit salad
4 oranges
2 tbsp icing sugar
2 tbsp orange blossom water
1 pomegranate (optional)
Few fresh mint leaves,
  to decorate

1. Preheat the oven to 180°C/fan 160°C/gas 4.
Grease and base-line a 23cm-round deep
springform cake tin with baking paper. Put the egg
yolks and 225g sugar in a large bowl. Using an
electric hand whisk, beat for a few minutes until
pale and thick. Fold in the almonds and zests. It
will be quite stiff at this stage.

2. In a separate large bowl, whisk the egg whites
with the extra sugar to soft peaks. Mix a little into
the almond mixture to loosen, then gently fold in
the rest until combined. Pour into the tin and bake
for 45 minutes, or until a skewer inserted into the
centre of the cake comes out clean. Cool in the tin
on a wire rack.

3. Meanwhile, make the syrup. Put the sugar and
fruit juices into a small pan with the spices and
leave over a low heat until the sugar has dissolved.
Bring to the boil and simmer for 5 minutes, until
syrupy. Strain into a bowl and cool slightly.

4. For the orange salad, slice the top and bottom off
each orange, then slice away the skin and pith. Cut
horizontally into thin slices and overlap on a serving
plate. Sprinkle over the sugar and orange water.

5. Cut the pomegranate, if using, in half and,
working over a bowl, tap the base of each half with
a rolling pin to knock out the seeds. Set aside.

6. Invert the cake on to a plate and pierce the base
all over with a fine skewer. Spoon over the syrup,
giving it time to soak in. Just before serving,
scatter the pomegranate seeds and mint over the
salad, and serve with slices of cake.

Orange and rosemary polenta cake

This gluten-free cake can be kept wrapped in the fridge for up to 5 days.

SERVES 8
TAKES 1½ HOURS, 1 HOUR BAKING,
PLUS COOLING

Butter, for greasing
2 large oranges
6 free-range eggs
150g polenta
150g ground almonds
250g golden caster sugar
1 tsp finely chopped fresh
  rosemary leaves
1 tsp demerara sugar

For the orange drizzle
100g caster sugar
3 tbsp orange liqueur,
  such as Grand Marnier,
  Cointreau or Triple Sec
1 tsp finely chopped fresh
  rosemary leaves
Grated or shredded zest
  of 1 orange

1. Grease and base-line a 23cm-round springform cake tin. Put the whole oranges in a large pan of water, bring to the boil and simmer for 1 hour, until soft. Remove, cool, then halve and remove the pips.

2. Preheat the oven to 180°C/fan 160°C/gas 4. Whiz the orange halves (with the skin) to a purée in a food processor. Beat in the eggs, polenta, almonds, sugar and rosemary.

3. Pour into the tin and sprinkle with the demerara sugar. Bake for 1 hour, until the cake is risen and golden.

4. For the drizzle, dissolve the sugar in 100ml hot water in a pan. Boil for 5 minutes but don't let it colour. Remove from the heat and cool briefly. Add the liqueur, rosemary and zest.

5. Cool the cake in the tin, then turn out and drizzle with the syrup.

Carrot cake

Carrot cake is an incredibly popular recipe. Who would have thought that one of your favourite desserts would be made from a common garden vegetable!

SERVES 10–12
TAKES 15 MINUTES, 45 MINUTES BAKING, PLUS COOLING

Butter, for greasing
100g raisins
4 tbsp sweet sherry or
  fresh orange juice
3 large free-range eggs
175ml sunflower oil
200g light muscovado sugar
2 tsp ground cinnamon
225g self-raising flour
½ tsp baking powder
½ tsp bicarbonate of soda
50g desiccated coconut
60g walnut pieces, plus extra
  to decorate
200g carrot, roughly grated
1 quantity cream cheese icing
  (see page 183)

1. Preheat the oven to 180°C/fan 160°C/gas 4. Grease a 22cm-round loose-bottomed cake tin with a little butter. Line the base of the tin with a circle of baking paper.

2. Place the raisins in a pan with the sherry or orange juice and bring to the boil. Simmer gently for 2 minutes until the raisins have absorbed all of the liquid. Set aside.

3. Put the eggs, sunflower oil and sugar in a large bowl, and whisk with an electric whisk for about 3 minutes, until the mixture becomes creamy.

4. Sift the cinnamon, flour, baking powder and bicarbonate of soda over the mixture, and fold it in with the coconut, walnuts, carrot and drained raisins. Spoon into the tin and bake for 45 minutes, or until a skewer pushed into the cake's centre comes out clean. Leave to cool in the tin, then transfer to a cooling rack to cool completely.

5. Spread the cream cheese icing over the top and sides of the cake and sprinkle with extra walnuts.

Coffee and walnut cake with tiramisu cream

Here the classic combination of coffee and walnut is given a new twist with this tiramisu cream.

SERVES 12
TAKES 20 MINUTES, 30 MINUTES
BAKING, PLUS COOLING AND ICING

225g butter, softened,
  plus extra for greasing
225g caster sugar
4 medium eggs
225g self-raising flour
3 tbsp coffee essence or strong
  black coffee made with instant
  coffee and a little boiling water
½ tsp baking powder
75g walnut pieces, finely
  chopped, plus walnut halves,
  to decorate
½ tsp each cocoa powder and
  icing sugar, to decorate

For the tiramisu cream
250g tub mascarpone
142ml carton double cream
4 tbsp coffee liqueur, such as
  Tia Maria
2 tsp caster sugar
Few drops of vanilla extract

1. Preheat the oven to 180°C/fan160°C/gas 4. Grease and base-line 2 x 20cm sandwich tins with butter and baking paper.

2. Beat the butter in a bowl with an electric hand whisk until soft and creamy. Add the caster sugar and beat until light and fluffy, then beat in the eggs, 1 at a time, adding a spoonful of flour with the second and last egg to prevent curdling. Beat in the coffee, sift over the remaining flour and baking powder, and fold in. Add the chopped walnuts.

3. Divide the mixture between the tins and lightly level them. Bake for 30 minutes, until well risen and golden and the tops spring back when lightly pressed. Leave to cool in the tins for 10 minutes, then turn out on to a wire rack and cool. (Freeze the cakes now, well wrapped in cling film, if you wish. Defrost thoroughly before icing.)

4. Make the tiramisu cream. Put the mascarpone in a bowl and gradually beat in the cream, followed by the coffee liqueur, caster sugar and vanilla extract.

5. Place 1 cake on a serving plate and spread with half of the tiramisu cream. Cover with the second cake and spread the top with the rest of the tiramisu cream. Mix the cocoa with the icing sugar and dust over the cake. Decorate with the walnut halves.

Variation For a traditional coffee and walnut cake, make 1 quantity of coffee buttercream (see page 182) to fill and top the cake. Decorate with walnut halves.

Poppy seed and lemon cake with cream cheese icing

This makes a nice change from a traditional lemon cake.
Serve plain and un-iced if you prefer something less sweet.

SERVES 8
TAKES 10 MINUTES, 1 HOUR
10 MINUTES BAKING, PLUS COOLING
AND DECORATING

175g butter, at room
  temperature, plus extra for
  greasing
175g caster sugar
Finely grated zest of 2 large
  lemons
3 medium eggs
250g self-raising flour
50g poppy seeds
4 heaped tbsp natural yogurt

For the crystallised rose petals
1 unsprayed pale yellow rose
Caster sugar, for dusting
1 egg white
½ quantity cream cheese
  icing (see page 183)

1. First make the crystallised rose petals. Carefully pull the petals off the rose. Fill a bowl with some sugar. Brush each petal with egg white, then bury under the sugar. Lift out, shake off the excess sugar and leave spaced out on a baking sheet to dry for a few hours or until brittle.

2. Preheat the oven to 150°C/fan 130°C/gas 2. Grease and base-line a 19cm x 12cm x 9cm deep loaf tin with baking paper. Put the butter into a bowl and beat with an electric hand whisk until creamy. Add the sugar and beat until it is almost white. Beat in the zest and eggs, 1 at a time, and a spoonful of flour with the second and last egg to prevent curdling. Sift over the rest of the flour and fold it in with the poppy seeds and the yogurt.

3. Spoon into the tin. Bake for 1 hour 10 minutes or until a skewer inserted into the centre of the cake comes out clean. Cool for 10 minutes, then turn out and cool on a wire rack.

4. Spread the cream cheese icing thickly over the cake and scatter with the crystallised petals.

Walnut, granola, honey and date cake

Use a crunchy toasted granola rather than a raw muesli for this moist afternoon-tea cake.

SERVES 8–10
TAKES 20 MINUTES, 1 HOUR BAKING, PLUS COOLING

150g softened butter
150ml honey
3 eggs, beaten
400g self-raising flour
½ tsp baking powder
200g crunchy granola
200ml milk
50g walnuts, chopped
100g ready-to-eat dried dates

For the yogurt icing
200g 0% fat Greek yogurt
1 tbsp honey
50g icing sugar
1 tsp vanilla extract
1 tbsp chopped walnuts,
   to decorate

1. Preheat the oven to 180°C/fan 160°C/gas 4. Grease and base-line a 900g loaf tin. Cream the softened butter with the honey in a mixing bowl until light. Add the beaten eggs, a little at a time, then sift over the flour and baking powder. Stir in the granola, milk, walnuts and dates. Stir to mix well, then pour into the loaf tin and bake for 1 hour, until golden and risen. Turn out on to a wire rack to cool.

2. Meanwhile, make the icing. Drain the yogurt in a sieve lined with muslin and suspended over a bowl. Leave for about 45 minutes.

3. Put the drained yogurt in a mixing bowl and beat in the honey, icing sugar and vanilla extract, and swirl over the cake. Sprinkle with chopped walnuts. The un-iced cake will keep in an airtight container for up to 3 days.

Coffee and pecan roulade

A fabulous dessert or even an afternoon-tea cake, this is far easier to make than it looks.

SERVES 6–8
TAKES 25 MINUTES, 20–22 MINUTES BAKING, PLUS COOLING

5 eggs
100g light brown soft sugar, plus extra to sprinkle
4 tbsp instant coffee powder
100g plain flour
1 tsp caster sugar, for sprinkling

For the pecan praline
150g chopped pecan nuts
250g caster sugar

For the filling and decoration
284ml carton double cream
1 tbsp icing sugar

1. Preheat the oven to 180°C/fan 160°C/gas 4. Line a Swiss-roll tin with baking paper. Beat the eggs and sugar together with an electric whisk for 5 minutes until thick and mousse-like and the mixture leaves a trail when the whisk is lifted.

2. Mix the coffee powder with 2 tablespoons hot water to make a paste. Sift the flour over the egg mixture and, using a large metal spoon, gently fold in with the coffee paste. Carefully spread in the tin. Bake for 12–14 minutes. Turn out on to baking paper sprinkled with a little caster sugar. Cool a little, then roll up from the long side with the paper. Cool.

3. Toast the pecans in the oven on a baking sheet lined with non-stick baking paper for 8 minutes. Dissolve the sugar in 4 tablespoons water in a heavy-based pan over a low heat. Turn up the heat and boil, without stirring, until the sugar begins to caramelise. When it's a deep chestnut colour, pour over the nuts and leave to set for 15 minutes. Break the praline into rough shards then pulse all of it in a food processor until it looks like rubble.

4. Whip the double cream with the icing sugar until it just holds its shape, then spread over the unrolled roulade. Sprinkle with half the praline and roll up. Decorate with the remaining praline.

Variation Use coffee- or cocoa-flavoured buttercream, or mascarpone and coffee liqueur in place of the filling. Or if you want a plain Swiss roll, simply leave out the coffee powder and fill with raspberry jam instead.

chocolate
cakes

Orange, almond and chocolate dessert cake

For a celebratory treat you really should try this luscious gateau. With lashings of dark-chocolate ganache it is wonderful served with a little pot of crème fraîche – truly a taste of decadence.

SERVES 12
TAKES 50 MINUTES, 1 HOUR
20 MINUTES BAKING, PLUS COOLING

2 oranges
150g plain chocolate
5 eggs
400g golden caster sugar
350g sunflower oil
125g ground almonds
25g cocoa powder
375g plain flour
1½ tsp baking powder
3–4 tbsp orange liqueur
1 quantity chocolate ganache
  (see page 183)
Crystallised orange peel,
  to decorate
Crème fraîche, to serve

1. Put the whole oranges in a large saucepan and cover with water. Bring to the boil and simmer gently for 30 minutes. Remove to a food processor with a slotted spoon and whiz to a purée, then allow to cool.

2. Meanwhile, preheat the oven to 180°C/fan 160°C/gas 4. Grease and base-line a deep 23–24cm-round cake tin. Melt the chocolate in a bowl set over a pan of simmering water. Remove from the heat, stir until smooth, then cool.

3. In a large bowl, lightly beat the eggs, sugar and oil. Gradually beat in the orange purée, then the chocolate. Sift the cocoa, flour and baking powder into a bowl, mix in the almonds and fold into the chocolate mixture. Spoon into the tin and level.

4. Bake for 1 hour 20 minutes (cover with foil if it gets too brown) – it's ready when a skewer inserted into the centre comes out clean. Turn out and cool on a wire rack. Drizzle the top of the cake with the orange liqueur.

5. To decorate: swirl the ganache over the cake using a palette knife. Decorate with strips of crystallised orange peel and serve with pots of crème fraîche.

Chocolate beetroot cake

Crazy as it sounds, beetroot makes this cake deliciously moist
– we dare you to try it.

SERVES 10–12
TAKES 20 MINUTES, 50 MINUTES–
1 HOUR IN THE OVEN, PLUS COOLING

100ml sunflower oil, plus extra
  for greasing
250g plain chocolate, broken up
3 large free-range eggs
200g light muscovado sugar
1 tsp vanilla extract
100g self-raising flour
½ tsp bicarbonate of soda
½ tsp baking powder
50g ground almonds
250g raw beetroot

For the icing
150g plain chocolate
100g icing sugar
100ml soured cream

1. Preheat the oven to 180°C/fan 160°C/gas 4. Grease a 22cm-round loose-bottomed cake tin with a little oil and base-line with baking paper.

2. Place the plain chocolate in a bowl and set over a pan of gently simmering water. Allow the chocolate to melt slowly until smooth, then set aside to cool.

3. Place the eggs, sugar and sunflower oil in a large mixing bowl and whisk together, using an electric hand whisk, for about 3 minutes until the mixture is smooth and creamy. Stir in the vanilla extract, then sift over the self-raising flour, bicarbonate of soda and baking powder, and gently fold in, together with the ground almonds.

4. Using a pair of rubber gloves to protect your fingers from staining, peel and grate the beetroot, then squeeze out the excess liquid. Fold the beetroot into the mixture with the cooled chocolate, until thoroughly mixed.

5. Pour the mixture into the prepared tin and bake for 50 minutes–1 hour. Cover with foil if the cake browns too quickly. Test the cake by inserting a skewer into the centre to see if it comes out clean. Cool, then remove from the tin and leave to cool completely on a wire rack.

6. For the icing, place the chocolate in a bowl set over a pan of gently simmering water. Allow to melt until smooth. Set aside to cool, then beat in the icing sugar and soured cream until you have a thick, creamy and spreadable icing. Spread it over the top and sides of the cooled cake and serve.

Chocolate rum and raisin torte

Give your guests a real treat with this dark and delicious dish made of chocolate, rum and raisins. It's divine.

SERVES 8–10

TAKES 30 MINUTES, 35–40 MINUTES BAKING, PLUS OVERNIGHT SOAKING AND COOLING

75g raisins

75g dark rum, plus 3 tbsp extra for ganache

100g butter, cubed, plus extra for greasing

200g plain chocolate, broken up

4 eggs, separated

100g caster sugar

55g plain flour

85g ground almonds

1 quantity chocolate ganache (see page 183)

Marrons glacés, to decorate (available from large delis and specialist food shops), halved

1 tsp cocoa powder, to dust

Whipped cream or ice cream, to serve

1. Place the raisins in a bowl, pour in the rum then cover and leave to soak overnight. They will absorb half of the rum and become very plump.

2. Preheat the oven to 180°C/fan 160°C/gas 4. Grease and base-line a 20cm-round loose-bottomed cake tin.

3. Put the chocolate in a bowl and set over a pan of gently simmering water. Allow to melt, stirring gently, until smooth – make sure the bowl doesn't touch the water. Gradually stir in the butter, a little at a time, until melted. Remove from the heat.

4. Beat the egg yolks and sugar until pale, then stir in the chocolate. Sift the flour over the chocolate mixture, then carefully fold in, along with the almonds, rum and raisins.

5. Whisk the egg whites until stiff but not dry, and fold into the chocolate mixture. Pour into the prepared tin and bake for 35–40 minutes. Set aside to cool in the tin for 10 minutes, then remove from the tin and leave to cool completely on a wire rack.

6. Meanwhile, make the ganache following the recipe on page 183, adding the extra rum to the cream mixture, stirring occasionally, until thickened to a good icing consistency – thick but not solid. Spread over the top and sides of the torte, then decorate with marrons glacés and dust with cocoa powder. Serve with whipped cream or ice cream.

★ DELICIOUS. TIP Marrons glacés (candied chestnuts) are a treat, especially when they're combined with chocolate and rum. Any leftovers will keep in an airtight container for up to 2 days.

Chocolate praline fancies

These little iced squares make a perfect afternoon-tea treat.

MAKES 16 FANCIES
TAKES 40 MINUTES, 25–30 MINUTES
BAKING, PLUS COOLING AND SETTING

170g butter, softened, plus
  extra for greasing
170g caster sugar
3 large eggs
140g self-raising flour
30g cocoa powder
50ml hazelnut liqueur
  (Frangelico) or you can
  substitute amaretto or Tia
  Maria (optional)
Gold leaf, to decorate (optional)

For the praline buttercream
340g icing sugar, sifted
2 tbsp hazelnut butter (available
  from most supermarkets)
50ml milk
60g butter, softened

For the fondant icing
200g fondant icing sugar, sifted
60g cocoa powder, sifted

1. Preheat the oven to 190°C/fan 170°C/gas 5.
Grease and base-line a 20cm-square cake tin. In a
bowl, cream together the butter and sugar until
light and fluffy. Add the eggs, 1 at a time, mixing
well after each addition. Sift in the flour and cocoa,
and fold in gently. Pour into the tin and smooth the
top. Bake for 25–30 minutes, or until a skewer
inserted into the centre comes out clean. Remove
from the tin and cool on a wire rack.

2. Meanwhile, make the praline buttercream. In a
bowl, mix the icing sugar, hazelnut butter, milk and
butter until light and creamy. Cover and set aside.

3. Trim the edges of the cooled cake with a sharp
knife. Slice horizontally into 3 layers; lift off each
layer using a flat baking sheet to keep them whole.

4. Put the bottom layer on a chopping board. Drizzle
with half the liqueur, if using, and spread with half
the buttercream. Put the middle cake layer on top
and repeat, using the remaining liqueur and most of
the buttercream – reserve 1 tablespoon. Add the final
layer. Put in the fridge to set; at least 1 hour.

5. Make the icing. Put the fondant icing sugar and
cocoa in a pan with 110ml water. Heat gently,
stirring. Remove from the heat and stand for
5 minutes. Cut the cake into 16 squares. Spoon a
small blob of buttercream on to each cake.

6. Put the cakes on a wire rack. Spoon the icing
over the cakes to cover. Top with a little gold leaf, if
you like, and leave to set for 1 hour.

Variation To make plain fancies, replace the cocoa powder
with 30g self-raising flour and the hazelnut liqueur with
milk. Omit the cocoa from the icing and use less water.

Fruity chocolate flapjacks

These fabulous oaty and fruity bars are a winner at any time of day, thanks to their energising mix of dried cranberries, cherries or blueberries.

CUTS INTO 12 BARS
TAKES 20 MINUTES, 25–30 MINUTES BAKING, PLUS COOLING

200g butter
150g golden syrup
450g rolled oats
75g light muscovado sugar
125g mixed dried berries, such as cranberries, cherries or blueberries
200g good-quality plain or milk chocolate, broken up

1. Preheat the oven to 190°C/fan 170°C/ gas 5. Melt the butter and golden syrup in a small saucepan over a low–medium heat. Remove from the heat.

2. Put the oats, sugar and berries in a mixing bowl and stir in the butter and syrup mixture. Tip into a non-stick 23cm-square x 6cm-deep cake tin, press in well and bake for 25–30 minutes, until golden and firm. Set aside to cool in the tin.

3. Meanwhile, melt the chocolate in a heatproof bowl over a pan of just-simmering water, making sure the bowl doesn't touch the water. Remove from the heat and stir until smooth. Pour over the top of the flapjack, spread evenly and put aside to cool and set. Cut into 12 slices, wrap in baking paper and store in an airtight container for up to 3 days.

Nuts about nutty tray bake

You'll go nuts for this irresistible recipe. Lovely to bake for a
party or just to enjoy with as many cups of tea as they'll stretch to.

MAKES 24 SLICES
TAKES 20 MINUTES, 25–30 MINUTES
BAKING, PLUS COOLING

120g dark muscovado sugar
70g butter
40g golden syrup
1 tbsp double cream
300g mixed nuts, toasted
  (we used cashew, walnut,
  macadamia and pistachio nuts)

For the base
225g plain flour
80g light muscovado sugar
100g butter, melted, plus extra
  for greasing
50g plain chocolate, melted

1. Preheat the oven to 180°C/fan 160°C/gas 4.
Grease a non-stick baking tin (about 17.5cm x 27cm
x 4cm deep).

2. Make the base. Sift the flour into a bowl, add
the sugar, then pour in the melted butter and
chocolate. Mix well, then press evenly into the base
of the cake tin. Bake for 15–20 minutes, then leave
to cool slightly.

3. Meanwhile, make the topping. Put the sugar,
butter and golden syrup into a pan over a medium
heat. Stir often to dissolve the sugar but don't let
the mixture boil. Add the cream and mix well. Add
the nuts and stir until they are covered with the
sauce. Spread evenly over the base in the tin and
bake for 10 minutes. Set aside to cool, then slice
and serve.

Chocolate and hazelnut truffles

This recipe is a new take on truffles; not only are they easier to make, but we think they taste nicer, too.

MAKES 36 TRUFFLES

TAKES 20 MINUTES, 15–20 MINUTES BAKING, PLUS COOLING AND CHILLING

50g butter, plus extra for greasing

Unsweetened cocoa powder, to dust

150g skinned hazelnuts

90g plain flour

100g golden caster sugar

½ tsp salt

500g sweet plain chocolate, such as Bournville, roughly chopped

2 large eggs

225ml double cream

1. Preheat the oven to 180°C/fan 160°C/gas 4. Grease the base and sides of a 20cm-square cake tin with a little butter. Dust all over with cocoa powder, knocking out the excess.

2. Whiz 100g of the hazelnuts, the flour, sugar and salt in a food processor until coarsely ground. Roughly chop the rest of the nuts and stir in. Melt the butter in a saucepan over a low heat, then add 150g of the chocolate. Let it melt slightly, then whisk until smooth. Remove from the heat, add the eggs, one at a time, whisking well between each addition. Stir in the nut mixture until well combined. Spoon into the tin and spread evenly. Bake for 15–20 minutes. Leave to cool in the tin.

3. To make the ganache, put the rest of the chocolate in a bowl. Bring the cream just to the boil in a pan over a low heat, and pour over the chocolate. Stir until melted and thickened. Spread over the cold hazelnut base. Tap the tin on the counter surface to smooth evenly. Cover with cling film and chill for 3 hours. Cut into squares with a warmed knife, wiping the knife after each cut.

4. To assemble your gift: put in a box, tied with a ribbon. Keep in an airtight container in the fridge for up to a week.

Variation These are just as delicious without the ganache. Cut the biscuits a little larger and serve as cakes rather than petits fours.

Chocolate chunk brownies

The classic, ultimate brownie with a moist, fudgy texture and an intense chocolate flavour. Serve warm with ice cream.

MAKES 16 SQUARES
TAKES 15 MINUTES, 25–30 MINUTES BAKING, PLUS COOLING

200g plain chocolate
  (70% cocoa solids) chopped
  into small pieces
125g unsalted softened butter
275g light muscovado sugar
1 tsp vanilla extract
2 large eggs, beaten
100g plain flour
2 tbsp cocoa powder

1 Preheat the oven to 180°C/fan 160°C/gas 4. Grease and base-line a 20cm-square cake tin with baking paper. Put half the chocolate into a heatproof bowl set over a pan of gently simmering water and allow to melt slowly. Remove the bowl from the heat and allow to cool while making the mixture.

2 Put the butter in a large mixing bowl and, using a wooden spoon or electric hand mixer, beat until soft and creamy. Add the sugar and vanilla extract, and continue beating until the mixture is soft and fluffy.

3 Gradually beat in the eggs then sift over the flour and cocoa. Spoon over the melted chocolate and stir everything together thoroughly. Stir in the rest of the chopped chocolate pieces and then pour the mixture into the prepared tin.

4 Bake in the preheated oven for 25–30 minutes until firm to the touch but still soft and gooey in the centre. The brownies will continue to cook as they cool. Leave to cool in the tin and then remove from the tin using the paper to lift them out and cut into 16 squares. Eat warm or at room temperature.

biscuits

Raspberry maple shortcakes

These shortcakes are delicious on their own or layered up with this rich maple syrup cream and served with tangy fresh raspberries.

SERVES 6
TAKES 30 MINUTES, 8–10 MINUTES BAKING, PLUS CHILLING AND COOLING

115g salted butter
60g caster sugar
175g plain flour, plus extra
  for dusting
2 tbsp maple syrup

For the maple sauce
250ml double cream
125ml maple syrup
2 tbsp light brown soft sugar

For the filling
284ml carton double cream
300g fresh raspberries
Icing sugar, for dusting

1. Preheat the oven to 190°C/fan 170°C/gas 5. Using a mixer or electric hand whisk, cream the butter and sugar until light and fluffy. Add the flour and maple syrup, and mix to form a ball of dough. Wrap in cling film and chill for 1 hour.

2. Meanwhile, make the maple sauce. Heat the cream, maple syrup and brown sugar in a pan over a low heat until the sugar has dissolved. Bring to a gentle boil, then reduce to a simmer for 5 minutes, until thickened. Set aside to cool.

3. On a lightly floured surface, roll out the dough to a 5mm thickness. Using a 7cm cookie cutter, cut the dough into 18 rounds. Place on 2–3 large non-stick baking sheets and bake for 8–10 minutes, until pale golden. Cool on a wire rack.

4. When ready to serve, whip the cream for the filling until it just forms stiff peaks. Swirl through half of the maple sauce. Place 1 biscuit in the centre of a plate, top with a generous spoonful of the maple cream and a few raspberries. Top with a second biscuit and add a further generous spoonful of maple cream and some more raspberries. Top with a third biscuit. Repeat with the remaining biscuits to make 6 raspberry stacks.

5. Dust each stack with icing sugar and drizzle around the remaining sauce. Serve immediately.

Oat, apple and cinnamon biscuits

These biscuits are a treat with adults and kids alike.

MAKES ABOUT 15 BISCUITS
TAKES 15 MINUTES, 12 MINUTES
BAKING, PLUS COOLING

100g unsalted butter, softened,
  plus extra for greasing
70g granulated sugar
50g light muscovado sugar
1 large egg
140g plain flour
50g porridge oats
1 tsp ground cinnamon
¼ tsp bicarbonate of soda
100g dried ready-to-eat apples,
  roughly chopped
Icing sugar, for dusting

1. Preheat the oven to 180°C/fan 160°C/gas 4.
Lightly grease 2–3 non-stick baking sheets.
Put the butter and sugars into a large bowl and
cream together using an electric hand whisk until
pale, light and fluffy. Gradually beat in the egg until
mixed together.

2. In a small bowl, combine the flour, oats,
cinnamon, bicarbonate of soda and a good pinch
of salt. Lightly fold this into the butter and egg
mixture, along with the dried apples, until just
combined into a dough.

3. Drop tablespoonfuls of the dough on to
the baking sheets, spaced apart to allow for some
spreading. Bake for 12 minutes, then remove from
the oven. Leave on the baking sheets for 2 minutes,
then transfer to a wire rack to cool. Dust with icing
sugar and eat immediately, or store in an airtight
container for up to 5 days.

Variation To ring the changes, make a batch
with raisins, dried apricots or a mix of dried
fruits instead of the apple.

Chocolate chip cookies

You'll catch many hands in the cookie jar if you bake these old favourites.

MAKES ABOUT 15 COOKIES
TAKES 15 MINUTES, 8–10 MINUTES BAKING, PLUS COOLING

115g unsalted butter, softened,
   plus extra for greasing
50g granulated sugar
70g light muscovado sugar
½ tsp vanilla extract
1 large egg, lightly beaten
160g plain flour
¼ tsp bicarbonate of soda
100g milk or Bournville
   chocolate, cut into chunks

1. Preheat the oven to 180°C/fan 160°C/gas 4. Lightly grease 2–3 non-stick baking sheets. Put the butter and sugars into a large bowl and cream together using an electric hand whisk until pale and fluffy. Gradually beat in the vanilla and egg.

2. In a small bowl, mix the flour, bicarbonate of soda and a good pinch of salt, then add to the creamed mixture, along with the chocolate chunks. Mix until combined to a softish dough.

3. Put tablespoonfuls of the dough on to the baking sheets, spaced well apart to allow for spreading. Bake for 8–10 minutes, then remove from the oven. Leave on the baking sheets for 2 minutes, then transfer to a wire rack to cool. Eat immediately or store in an airtight container for up to 5 days.

Double chocolate toffee cookie

A giant chewy cookie fit for all occasions.

MAKES 1 LARGE COOKIE TO SERVE 8
TAKES 20 MINUTES, 30–35 MINUTES
BAKING, PLUS COOLING

115g unsalted butter, softened,
  plus extra for greasing
50g granulated sugar
70g light muscovado sugar
1 large egg, lightly beaten
140g plain flour
15g cocoa powder
¼ tsp bicarbonate of soda
50g white chocolate, cut into
  chunks
50g milk chocolate, cut into
  chunks
100g toffees, cut into chunks
50g white icing sugar, for the
  glacé icing

1. Preheat the oven to 180°C/fan 160°C/gas 4. Lightly grease and base-line a shallow, 24cm loose-bottomed fluted tart tin with baking paper. Put the butter and sugars into a large bowl, and cream together using an electric hand whisk until pale, light and fluffy. Gradually beat in the egg.

2. In a small bowl, sift together the flour, cocoa powder and bicarbonate of soda, then stir in a good pinch of salt. Lightly mix into the creamed mixture, along with the chocolate and toffee pieces, until just combined into a softish dough.

3. Press the dough into the prepared tart tin with your fingers. Bake for 30–35 minutes, until the edges are darker and the centre is almost set. Remove from the oven and allow to cool for 20 minutes in the tin (otherwise it will crack as you try to remove it). Remove from the tin and cool completely on a wire rack. Peel off and discard the baking paper.

4. Sift the icing sugar into a small bowl and mix to a fairly thin icing with 2 teaspoons of water. For a general occasion, drizzle lines of icing across the cookie using a metal spoon. For a special occasion, such as a birthday, spoon the icing into a piping bag fitted with a small plain nozzle, then pipe a message on to the cookie.

Peanut butter and cranberry biscuits

If you like peanut butter and jam sandwiches you will love these slightly crumbly biscuits.

MAKES ABOUT 30 BISCUITS
TAKES 20 MINUTES, 18–20 MINUTES
BAKING, PLUS COOLING

100g butter, softened, plus
  extra for greasing (optional)
250g crunchy peanut butter
250g light brown soft sugar
1 large free-range egg
Few drops of vanilla extract
125g oats
90g dried cranberries
125g plain flour
1 tsp bicarbonate of soda

1. Preheat the oven to 160°C/fan 140°C/ gas 3. Cut baking paper to fit 3 baking sheets or rub a little butter over the sheets. If you don't have 3 sheets, just cook 1 sheet at a time.

2. Beat the softened butter and peanut butter in a bowl with a wooden spoon. Add the sugar and beat again until well mixed.

3. Crack the egg into a bowl and whisk with a fork. Add the vanilla and egg to the peanut butter mixture, and beat again with the wooden spoon. Add the oats and cranberries to the mixture, sift over the flour and bicarbonate of soda, and mix well.

4. Put large spoonfuls of the mixture on to the sheets, spacing slightly apart, and bake for 18–20 minutes until light golden. Remove from the oven. Leave to firm up on their sheets for a few minutes, then transfer to wire racks to cool completely. When they are cool, make a little stack of the biscuits, wrap them in Cellophane and tie with a ribbon. Store in an airtight container in a cool place for up to 3 days.

★ DELICIOUS. TIP Freeze the uncooked dough in a log shape, wrapped in cling film, for up to 1 month. Slice into rounds, then bake from frozen at 160°C/fan 140°C/gas 3 for 22–25 minutes.

Variation Make these biscuits even nuttier by adding chopped salted or unsalted peanuts instead of the cranberries.

Chocolate peanut crumble cookies

Chocolate and peanut is a divine combination in these buttery cookies. They will keep for up to 4 days in an airtight container in the fridge or up to 2 months in the freezer.

MAKES 15 COOKIES

TAKES 20 MINUTES, 10–12 MINUTES BAKING, PLUS COOLING

115g salted butter, plus extra for greasing
115g caster sugar
1 heaped tbsp smooth peanut butter
1 large egg, lightly beaten
150g plain flour
30g cocoa powder
½ tsp bicarbonate of soda
100g plain chocolate chips
50g white chocolate

For the crumble topping
30g salted butter
40g plain flour
30g caster sugar
60g unsalted peanuts, half roughly chopped

1. Preheat the oven to 190°C/fan 170°C/gas 5 and grease 2 baking sheets.

2. Make the crumble topping. In a large mixing bowl, rub the butter into the flour and sugar with your fingertips, until a soft, crumbly dough is formed. Add the chopped and whole peanuts, then set aside.

3. Make the biscuit dough. In a separate mixing bowl, cream the butter, sugar and peanut butter. Add the egg and beat again. Sift in the flour, cocoa and bicarbonate of soda, and add the chocolate chips. Mix well to form a soft dough.

4. Roll the mixture into 15 small balls and divide between the baking trays, spacing well apart. Press each cookie down and top with a little crumble mix. Bake for 10–12 minutes until the crumble topping is golden, then remove from the oven and leave for 5 minutes before transferring to a cooling rack.

5. Melt the white chocolate in a heatproof bowl set over a pan of simmering water; stir occasionally until smooth. Drizzle the chocolate backwards and forwards over each cookie, then allow to cool and set before serving.

Variation Drizzle with dark chocolate, if you prefer, or a mixture of dark and white.

Snowballs

These little white snowballs really are something special –
they're simple to make and melt-in-the-mouth good.

MAKES 28 SNOWBALLS
TAKES 10 MINUTES, 10–12 MINUTES
BAKING, PLUS COOLING AND CHILLING

100g butter, softened, plus
  extra for greasing
150g icing sugar
150g plain flour
25g chopped walnuts
25g chopped almonds
Grated zest of 1 lemon

1. Preheat the oven to 180°C/fan 160°C/gas 4.
Cream the butter and 75g of the icing sugar until
soft and fluffy. Stir in the flour. Add the nuts, a good
pinch of salt and the lemon zest, and mix together
until they form a dough. Knead lightly. Cover in
cling film and chill for 30 minutes.

2. Roll into walnut-sized balls and bake on a lightly
greased baking sheet for 10–12 minutes. Allow to
cool slightly then tip into a large bowl containing
the rest of the icing sugar and toss to coat. Leave
to cool completely.

3. To give as a gift, when well cooled, pile into a
large jar with a screw top and decorate with ribbon.

★ DELICIOUS. TIP Feel free to make these ahead
of time. They'll keep in an airtight container for up
to 1 week.

bread and savoury baking

Basic white rustic loaf

This baking staple is a cinch to make. It's best eaten on the same day or used for toasting the following day.

MAKES ABOUT A 750G LOAF/12 SLICES
TAKES 15 MINUTES, 20–25 MINUTES
BAKING, PLUS PROVING AND COOLING

**500g strong white bread flour,
plus extra for dusting**
1 tsp fine salt
7g sachet fast-action dried yeast
**1 tbsp olive oil, plus extra for
greasing**

1. Sift the flour and salt into a large bowl. Stir in the yeast. Make a well in the centre and gradually mix in 300ml warm water and the oil until the dough comes together – add a dash more water if it seems dry.

2. Tip out on to a lightly floured surface and knead the dough for 5 minutes, until smooth. Shape like a rugby ball and put on to an oiled large baking sheet. Set aside in a warm place for 40 minutes or until doubled in size. (This is known as proving or rising.)

3. Preheat the oven to 220°C/fan 200°C/gas 7. Make deep slashes with a sharp knife in the top of the dough and dust with flour. Bake for 20–25 minutes, until risen, golden and cooked. To test if it's ready, tap the base of the loaf – it should sound hollow. Cool on a wire rack and slice to serve.

Cherry and pecan plait

Have a go at this lovely fruity and nutty bread – slices of it are perfect with a nice cup of tea.

CUTS INTO 12 SLICES
TAKES 30 MINUTES, 20–25 MINUTES BAKING, PLUS PROVING AND COOLING

500g strong white bread flour, plus extra for dusting
1 tsp caster sugar
2 tsp ground cinnamon
7g sachet fast-action dried yeast
1 tbsp maple syrup, plus extra for brushing
A little oil, for greasing
75g dried cherries
100g chopped pecan nuts
5 tbsp icing sugar

1. Sift the flour, ½ teaspoon salt, sugar and cinnamon into a large bowl. Stir in the yeast. Make a well in the centre and gradually mix in 300ml warm water and the maple syrup until the dough comes together – add a dash more water if it seems dry.

2. Tip out on to a lightly floured surface and knead the dough for 5 minutes until smooth. Shape into a ball and place in an oiled bowl, cover and set aside in a warm place for 1 hour or until doubled in size (this is known as proving or rising).

3. Knead the dried cherries and pecans into the risen dough. Divide into 3 equal pieces, roll each into a long sausage. Plait together the three pieces, then tuck the ends under. Put on to an oiled large baking sheet. Cover and set aside in a warm place for 45 minutes or until doubled in size.

4. Preheat the oven to 220°C/fan 200°C/gas 7. Brush the risen plait with a little extra maple syrup. Bake for 20–25 minutes, until risen, golden and cooked. To test if it's ready, tap the base of the loaf – it should sound hollow. Cool on a wire rack.

5. Mix the icing sugar with a few drops of water until it is smooth, then drizzle over the cooled bread. Slice and serve.

Brown knot rolls with pumpkin seeds

There's nothing nicer than homemade bread at a dinner party, so impress your guests with these sophisticated yet simple rolls.

MAKES ABOUT 8 ROLLS
TAKES 15 MINUTES, 15 MINUTES
BAKING, PLUS PROVING AND COOLING

500g strong brown or Granary
  bread flour, plus extra
  for dusting
1 tsp fine salt
7g sachet fast-action dried yeast
1 tbsp olive oil, plus extra
  for greasing
1 tbsp milk, for brushing
1 tbsp pumpkin seeds,
  to sprinkle

1. Sift the flour and salt into a large bowl. Stir in the yeast. Make a well in the centre and gradually mix in 300ml warm water and the oil until the dough comes together – add a dash more water if it seems dry.

2. Tip out on to a lightly floured surface and knead the dough for 5 minutes, until smooth. Divide the dough into 8 equal pieces. Roll each piece into a long sausage shape, then tie in a knot, tucking the ends neatly underneath. Place on a large oiled baking sheet, spacing well apart. Cover and set aside in a warm place for 30 minutes or until doubled in size (this is known as proving or rising).

3. Preheat the oven to 220°C/fan 200°C/gas 7. Brush the risen rolls with milk and scatter with pumpkin seeds. Bake for about 15 minutes, until risen, golden and cooked. To test if they are ready, tap the base of the rolls – they should sound hollow. Cool on a wire rack.

Feta, tomato and rosemary flowerpot bread

These are easy to make and so cute, either to serve for a special alfresco dinner party or to take on a picnic.

MAKES 8 ROLLS
TAKES 25 MINUTES, 20–25 MINUTES
BAKING, PLUS PROVING AND COOLING

240g tub SunBlush tomatoes
Olive oil, for greasing
500g strong white bread flour,
  plus extra for dusting
1 tsp fine salt
7g sachet fast-action dried yeast
2 tbsp finely chopped fresh
  rosemary leaves, plus a few
  extra sprigs
200g feta, crumbled

1. Drain the SunBlush tomatoes, reserving 1 tablespoon oil and 8 tomatoes. Chop the rest. Oil and flour 8 x 7cm clean terracotta pots.

2. Sift the flour and salt into a large bowl. Stir in the yeast and chopped rosemary. Make a well in the centre and gradually mix in 250ml warm water, 1 tablespoon of the SunBlush tomato oil and the chopped tomatoes, until the dough comes together. Add a dash more water if it seems dry.

3. Tip out on to a lightly floured surface and knead in 150g of the crumbled feta cheese. Knead the dough for 5 minutes, until smooth. Divide into 8 equal pieces, shape each into a ball and place in the flowerpots. Cover and set aside in a warm place for 30 minutes or until doubled in size (this is known as proving or rising).

4. Preheat the oven to 220°C/fan 200°C/gas 7. Top the dough with a little more feta and a reserved tomato, and push in a sprig of rosemary. Bake for 20–25 minutes, until risen, golden and cooked. Cool and serve warm or at room temperature.

Olive and thyme foccacia

This classic Italian bread is delicious served warm with a little balsamic vinegar and olive oil.

MAKES 1 LOAF TO SERVE 8
TAKES 15 MINUTES, 20–25 MINUTES
BAKING, PLUS PROVING AND COOLING

500g strong white bread flour,
  plus extra for dusting
1 tsp fine salt
7g sachet fast-action dried yeast
3–4 tbsp olive oil, plus extra
  for greasing
100g pitted black olives, chopped
Sea salt and 2 tbsp fresh thyme
  leaves, to sprinkle

1. Sift the flour and salt into a large bowl. Stir in the yeast. Make a well in the centre and gradually mix in 300ml warm water and 2 tablespoons oil until the dough comes together. Add a dash more water if it seems dry.

2. Tip out on to a lightly floured surface and knead the dough for 5 minutes, until smooth. Put on to an oiled, large baking sheet. Cover and set aside in a warm place for 1½ hours or until doubled in size (this is known as proving or rising).

3. Turn out the dough and knead in the olives. Shape the dough into a large circle and place on an oiled baking sheet. Prove again for 45 minutes.

4. Preheat the oven to 220°C/fan 200°C/gas 7. Press your fingertips into the risen and proved dough all over, drizzle with the remaining oil, scatter with sea salt and thyme. Bake for 20–25 minutes, until risen, golden and cooked. To test if it's ready, tap the base of the loaf – it should sound hollow. Drizzle with oil, cool slightly and serve warm.

Milk bread

This is a lovely old-fashioned white bread recipe.
Spread thick slices with butter and jam or toast it.

MAKES 1 LARGE LOAF
TAKES 20 MINUTES, 30 MINUTES
BAKING, PLUS PROVING AND COOLING

750g strong white bread flour,
  plus extra for dusting
2 tsp salt
75g butter, cut into small pieces,
  plus extra for greasing
7g sachet fast-action dried yeast
1 tbsp golden caster sugar
300ml milk

1. Put the flour into a large bowl and add the salt. Add the butter and rub it into the flour with your fingertips until it's like breadcrumbs. Tip in the yeast and sugar.

2. Pour the milk into a large measuring jug and stir in 150ml water. Microwave on High for 2 minutes until warm, or warm in a pan over a medium heat. Add to the flour and stir with a wooden spoon. Use your hands to mix until it forms a soft dough that leaves the sides of the bowl clean.

3. Sprinkle a work surface with flour, then tip the dough out on to it. Stretch and work the dough for 10 minutes until smooth and elastic. Roll the dough into an oblong shape.

4. Preheat the oven to 220°C/fan 200°C/gas 7. Grease a 900g loaf tin and add the dough. Cover with greased cling film and leave to rise in a warm place for about 25 minutes, until the dough is almost at the top (this is known as proving or rising). Discard the cling film, dust with some extra flour and bake for 30 minutes, until risen and golden brown. Cool in the tin for at least 20 minutes before removing and serving.

Cardamom-scented Chelsea buns

The addition of aromatic, heady cardamom makes these buns irresistible – at any time of day.

MAKES 9 BUNS
TAKES 35 MINUTES, 25–30 MINUTES
BAKING, PLUS PROVING AND COOLING

50g unsalted butter, diced,
  plus extra for greasing
450g strong white bread flour,
  plus extra for dusting
½ tsp salt
7g sachet fast-action dried yeast
25g golden caster sugar
1 medium egg
225ml warm milk
2 tsp clear honey
2 tbsp roughly chopped shelled
  pistachio nuts

For the filling
50g butter, softened
1 tsp roughly crushed
  cardamom seeds
50g sultanas
50g currants
50g light muscovado sugar

1. Grease a deep 23cm-square baking tin with butter. Sift the flour and salt into a large bowl. Rub in the butter until it resembles fine breadcrumbs, then stir in the yeast.

2. In another bowl, whisk the sugar and egg together. Add to the dry ingredients with all but 2 tablespoons of the milk. Mix to a soft dough, adding the remaining milk, if needed.

3. Turn out on to a lightly floured surface and knead for 15 minutes, until smooth and elastic. Put in a lightly greased bowl, cover with cling film and leave in a warm place to rise for 1 hour or until doubled in size (this is known as proving or rising).

4. Punch the dough in the bowl to 'knock back'. Tip back out on to the floured surface and, using a rolling pin, roll out into a rectangle about 25cm x 35cm.

5. Assemble the filling. Spread the butter over the dough, then scatter over the cardamom, dried fruit and sugar. Roll up like a Swiss roll from the long end and cut into 9 rounds. Arrange in the tin, cut-side down; 3 to a row. Cover with lightly greased cling film and put in a warm place for 45 minutes, until well risen.

6. Preheat the oven to 200°C/fan 180°C/gas 6. Bake the buns for 25–30 minutes or until golden. Remove from the oven and brush with the honey and sprinkle with the pistachios. Cool in the tin for about 10 minutes, then eat warm or transfer to a wire rack to cool completely.

Cornish saffron festival loaf

You can make 6 individual buns of this rich tea bread, instead of a whole loaf, if you prefer.

MAKES 1 LOAF
TAKES 35 MINUTES, 25 MINUTES
BAKING, PLUS INFUSING, PROVING
AND COOLING

25g butter, softened, plus
  extra for greasing and to
  serve (optional)
125ml milk, plus extra (optional)
2–3 large pinches of saffron
  strands
3 tbsp Cornish clotted cream,
  plus extra to serve (optional)
225g strong white bread flour,
  plus extra for dusting
7g sachet fast-action dried yeast
25g golden caster sugar
½ tsp ground mixed spice
25g sultanas
25g raisins
1 tbsp clear honey

1. Grease a long, thin 500g loaf tin with butter and set aside. Heat the milk in a small pan over a low heat until just below simmering point. Stir in the saffron strands and leave to infuse for about 15 minutes off the heat.

2. Add the cream to the milk and saffron in the pan, and return to a low heat. Warm (but don't boil) for 2 minutes. Meanwhile, sift the flour and ¼ teaspoon salt into a large bowl. Stir in the yeast, sugar and mixed spice. Make a well in the centre and add the warm milk mixture. Mix well to make a soft dough, adding extra milk if needed.

3. Turn out on to a floured surface and knead for 15 minutes, adding the softened butter and dried fruit as you go, until the dough is soft and elastic. Pop into a lightly oiled bowl and cover with cling film. Leave in a warm place for 1 hour or until doubled in size (this is known as proving or rising).

4. Punch the dough in the bowl to 'knock back', then turn out on to a floured surface and knead for 5 minutes. Split the dough into 3 even pieces and roll out into long 'sausages', just a little longer than the tin. Plait the dough together and tuck the ends under as you lift it into the tin. Cover with some lightly greased cling film and leave in a warm place for at least 1½ hours or until doubled in size again.

5. Preheat the oven to 180°C/fan 160°C/gas 4. Bake for 25 minutes, until risen and golden. Remove from the oven and brush with the honey. Leave to cool in the tin for 5–10 minutes, then turn out on to a wire rack to cool completely. Cut into thick slices and spread with clotted cream or butter, if you like.

Basil and goat's cheese cornbread

This is great served either just warm or cold, and any leftovers (unlikely) are especially good lightly toasted. Serve with a mixture of salads at a picnic or barbecue.

SERVES 6–8

TAKES 15 MINUTES, 40 MINUTES BAKING, PLUS COOLING

Oil, for greasing

150g yellow cornmeal or polenta (do not use 'instant' polenta)

100g plain flour

2 tsp baking powder

1 tbsp caster sugar

15g fresh basil leaves, chopped

1–2 red chillies, seeded and finely chopped

40g freshly grated Parmesan

250ml buttermilk (or an equal mixture of soured cream and skimmed milk)

2 large eggs, beaten

2 tbsp extra-virgin olive oil

100–130g soft goat's cheese, diced or crumbled

1. Preheat the oven to 220°C/fan 200°C/gas 7. Grease a 22cm x 11cm x 7cm loaf tin (or line with non-stick baking paper).

2. Mix together the cornmeal or polenta, flour, 1 teaspoon salt, a good grinding of black pepper, baking powder and sugar in a bowl. Add the chopped basil, chillies and Parmesan. Mix. Beat together the buttermilk (or soured cream and milk), eggs and olive oil. Mix the liquid into the dry ingredients quickly and briefly. Do not overmix, but make sure that everything is thoroughly blended. Stir in the goat's cheese.

3. Pour into the prepared tin and bake for about 40 minutes, until the bread is risen, golden and a skewer inserted into the centre comes out clean (turn the heat down a notch after 30 minutes if the top starts to brown too much).

4. Cool in the tin for 10 minutes, then turn out and leave to cool on a wire rack.

Spinach and goat's cheese muffins

These fluffy savoury muffins are an easy and versatile
American-style bun – especially good for a light lunch.

MAKES 9 MUFFINS
TAKES 20 MINUTES, 20–25 MINUTES
BAKING, PLUS COOLING

25g butter, plus extra for
  greasing
200ml milk
100g baby leaf spinach
250g plain flour
1 tbsp baking powder
1 tsp bicarbonate of soda
Good pinch of cayenne pepper
50g fresh Parmesan, finely
  grated
1 egg, lightly beaten
200g rindless soft goat's
  cheese

1. Preheat the oven to 190°C/fan 170°C/gas 5.
Lightly grease 9 holes of a deep muffin tin with a
little butter.

2. Place the milk and butter in a large pan over a
high heat. When the butter has melted, stir in the
spinach and bring just to the boil. Remove from the
heat and pour into a liquidiser or food processor.
Whiz until the spinach is finely chopped. Allow to
cool for 5 minutes.

3. Sift the flour, baking powder and bicarbonate of
soda into a large bowl. Add the cayenne and some
freshly ground black pepper. Stir in the Parmesan.
Add the egg and the spinach mixture, then beat
with a wooden spoon until just mixed. Divide
among 9 muffin holes, filling each about half full.

4. Add a little goat's cheese to each muffin hole.
Top with the remaining mixture, followed by a little
more cheese, pushing the cheese down into the
mixture. Bake for 20–25 minutes, until risen and
firm to the touch. Leave to cool for 5 minutes, then
turn out on to a wire rack. Serve hot or cold.

★ DELICIOUS. TIP Allow the milk to cool a little
before you add it to the dry ingredients or the baking
powder will start working before it gets into the
oven. Don't be tempted to use goat's cheese with
rind on – it doesn't melt nicely. These muffins taste
best when eaten within 24 hours, but you can freeze
them, wrapped in a plastic bag, for up to 1 month.

Carrot and coriander muffins

These veggie muffins are large American-style buns. Although we usually associate muffins with sweet fruits like blueberries, this is an easy, savoury recipe. Quicker to make than scones and perfect to eat with cheese or ham and pickle.

MAKES 9 MUFFINS
TAKES 20 MINUTES, 20–25 MINUTES BAKING, PLUS COOLING

2 tsp cumin seeds
175g carrots
50g pumpkin seeds
2 tbsp chopped fresh coriander
150g plain flour
100g wholemeal flour
1 tbsp baking powder
1 tsp bicarbonate of soda
200ml milk
1 egg, lightly beaten
4 tbsp olive oil
Crumbly cheese and chutney, to serve (optional)

1. Preheat the oven to 190°C/fan 170°C/gas 5. Use 9cm x 10cm squares of baking paper to line 9 holes of a deep muffin tin. Put the cumin seeds in a frying pan and dry-fry over a high heat for a minute, until toasted. Tip into a large bowl.

2. Peel and coarsely grate the carrots and add to the bowl, along with the pumpkin seeds and coriander. Sift in both flours, the baking powder, bicarbonate of soda, ½ teaspoon salt and a little black pepper. Gently mix with the carrot.

3. Stir in the milk, egg and olive oil. Beat lightly with a wooden spoon until just mixed. Divide among the 9 lined muffin holes, filling each one about two-thirds full. Bake for 20–25 minutes, until risen and firm to the touch. Cool for 5 minutes, then turn out on to a wire rack. Serve hot or cold with crumbly cheese and chutney, if you like.

★ DELICIOUS. TIP These taste best eaten the day they are made. You can freeze them though, wrapped in a plastic bag, for up to 1 month.

Ham, cheese and mustard muffins

Your party guests will love these oh-so-tiny but oh-so-tasty mini muffins.

MAKES 40–45 MUFFINS
TAKES 25 MINUTES, 8–10 MINUTES BAKING, PLUS COOLING

225g self-raising flour
1 tsp baking powder
3 slices oak-smoked ham, chopped
6 fresh sage leaves, finely chopped
75g mature Cheddar, chopped
50g unsalted butter, melted and cooled slightly
1 medium egg, lightly beaten
1½ tbsp wholegrain mustard
150ml semi-skimmed milk

1. Preheat the oven to 200°C/fan 180°C/gas 6. Sift the flour, baking powder and a good pinch of salt into a large bowl. Stir in the ham, sage and Cheddar. Make a well in the centre, then add the butter, egg, mustard and milk. Mix together briefly, until just combined.

2. Put teaspoonfuls of the mixture into petits fours cases, so that each is about three-quarters full. Place on 2 large baking sheets and bake for 8–10 minutes, until risen and golden. Transfer to wire racks to cool a little.

3. To serve, peel off the petits fours cases and line the muffins up on serving plates. Serve warm or at room temperature. Put your favourite chutney into a serving bowl for guests to dunk the muffins in.

★ DELICIOUS. TIP Make the muffins, then cool and freeze in food bags for up to 1 month. Defrost in the fridge overnight, then serve at room temperature.

Cheese and mustard scones

Try these deliciously cheesy scones – they're ideal for a picnic or for a lunchbox.

MAKES 12 SCONES
TAKES 20 MINUTES, 12–15 MINUTES BAKING, PLUS COOLING

250g self-raising flour
1 tsp baking powder
½ tsp English mustard powder
Large pinch of cayenne pepper
1 tsp light muscovado sugar
70g butter, slightly softened
  and cut into small pieces
100g mature Cheddar, grated
25g Parmesan, grated
150ml buttermilk
½ tsp English mustard
1 tbsp milk

1. Preheat the oven to 200°C/fan 180°C/gas 6. Sift the flour, baking powder, mustard and cayenne into a bowl and add ½ teaspoon of salt, a good grind of black pepper and the sugar. Add the butter and rub into the flour using your fingertips. Mix 70g of the Cheddar and all the Parmesan into the mixture, then bind together with enough buttermilk to make a soft, non-sticky dough.

2. Roll the mixture to about 1.5cm thick and press out 12 scones (5–6cm diameter), re-rolling the dough as necessary. Place on a baking sheet lined with parchment.

3. Beat the mustard with the milk, and brush over the scones. Top each with a little of the remaining Cheddar. Bake for 12–15 minutes until well-risen and golden brown. Cool a little on a wire tray. Serve warm, spread with butter.

Variation For bacon scones, replace the Cheddar with 2–3 chopped fried bacon rashers and 1 teaspoon chopped fresh thyme leaves.

Pesto, mascarpone and tomato pastry wheels

These nifty vegetarian nibbles are simply amazing. Just roll them out and watch them go.

MAKES 28 WHEELS
TAKES 15 MINUTES, 18–20 MINUTES BAKING, PLUS FREEZING AND COOLING

25g pine nuts
2 garlic cloves, roughly chopped
50g fresh basil leaves
4 tbsp olive oil
25g vegetarian Parmesan, grated
375g pack fresh ready-rolled shortcrust pastry, brought up to room temperature
125g mascarpone
100g sun-dried tomatoes, chopped

1. Put the pine nuts into a blender with the garlic, basil leaves and oil. Whiz to a rough-textured pesto. Season with freshly ground black pepper, add the Parmesan and pulse briefly to combine. Set aside.

2. Unroll the pastry and spread evenly with the mascarpone. Top with the sun-dried tomatoes and dot evenly with the pesto. Starting with 1 long edge, roll the pastry tightly like a Swiss roll. Freeze for 30 minutes.

3. Preheat the oven to 200°C/fan 180°C/gas 6. Using a large serrated knife, slice the pastry into 28 thin rounds. Divide between 2 non-stick baking sheets, spaced slightly apart, and cover each sheet with foil – this will stop the sun-dried tomatoes turning too dark in the oven. Bake for 15 minutes, then uncover and bake for 3–5 minutes more, until cooked, crisp and pale-golden. Transfer to a wire rack to cool slightly.

4. Overlap the pastry wheels in a circle on a large, round serving plate. Serve them warm or at room temperature.

★ DELICIOUS. TIP Once cooked, you can freeze these for up to 1 month. Defrost at room temperature and reheat in the oven at 200°C/fan 180°C/gas 6 for 5 minutes.

seasonal baking

The biggest hot cross bun

Homemade hot cross buns are delicious, but as all that shaping takes time, try this one-mix, one-knead, one-rise bun. It couldn't be easier.

MAKES 1 LARGE LOAF TO SERVE 8
TAKES 30 MINUTES, 40 MINUTES
BAKING, PLUS PROVING AND COOLING

425g strong white bread
  flour, plus 1 tbsp and
  extra for dusting
50g butter, cubed
7g sachet fast-action dried
  yeast
1 tsp ground mixed spice
50g light muscovado sugar
200g luxury mixed dried fruit
125ml milk, plus 1 tbsp
  for brushing

1. Put the flour and ½ teaspoon salt in a mixing bowl. Add the butter and rub into the flour until it resembles breadcrumbs. Stir in the yeast, then add the remaining ingredients, except the milk.

2. Pour the 125ml milk into a jug and add 125ml boiling water. Stir into the dough and mix until it comes together as a soft ball. Turn the dough out on to a lightly floured work surface and knead for 10 minutes, until smooth and elastic. Form into a ball and put on a non-stick baking sheet. Cover and leave in a warm place for about 1 hour or until the dough doubles in size and feels very light and airy (this is known as proving or rising).

3. Preheat the oven to 200°C/fan 180°C/gas 6. Brush the top of the bun with the remaining milk. To make the cross, mix 1 tablespoon flour and 1 tablespoon water to make a soft paste for piping. Put into a disposable piping bag, snip the end and pipe a cross over the dough.

4. Bake the hot cross bun in the oven for 40 minutes or until golden brown. To test if it's cooked, carefully turn the bun over and tap the base – it's ready if it sounds hollow. Cook for a further 10 minutes if necessary. Transfer to a wire rack to cool. The hot cross bun is best eaten within 24 hours with butter or, after that, toasted and spread with butter.

Mini simnel cakes

Try these special little cakes made with luxury dried fruit and marzipan – they're delicious!

MAKES 12 CAKES
TAKES 40 MINUTES, 40 MINUTES
BAKING, PLUS COOLING

175g butter, softened, plus
  extra for greasing
175g caster sugar
3 medium eggs
225g plain flour, sifted
1 tsp baking powder
1 tsp ground mixed spice
350g luxury mixed dried fruit
100g chopped walnuts or
  blanched almonds
Grated zest and juice of
  1 orange
100g natural almond paste,
  cubed

For the decoration
Icing sugar, to dust
325g natural almond paste
Yellow and green food paste
  colours

1. Preheat the oven to 160°C/fan 140°C/gas 3 and lightly grease a 12 x 125ml muffin tin or mould. Beat the butter, sugar, eggs and flour in a mixing bowl until smooth. Add the baking powder, spice, fruit and nuts, orange zest and juice, and mix well. Divide among the muffin holes and push in the almond paste pieces. Bake for 40 minutes or until golden and firm. Cool for 20 minutes, then remove from the tin and set aside on a wire rack.

2. To decorate, dust a work surface with icing sugar. Thinly roll out 250g of the almond paste. Press out 12 rounds with a 7cm plain cutter (re-roll the trimmings). Press on each cake and crimp the edges.

3. Colour 50g of the remaining almond paste with yellow colouring, kneading to distribute evenly. Repeat with the remaining 25g of paste and the green colouring. Roll out the yellow paste and cut out 12 primroses with a flower cutter (from cake-decorating shops) or using a small knife. Roll 12 small balls from the trimmings for the centre of each flower.

4. Using the green almond paste, roll out 12 tiny sausages. Flatten and shape each to make leaves. Mark veins on each with the back of a knife. Put beside each primrose and put on top of each cake to serve.

Rose-petal chocolate cake

What would Easter be without chocolate? Give your friends a real treat with this deluxe chocolate cake that's brimming with sweet sherry.

SERVES 10–12

TAKES 40 MINUTES, 1¼–1½ HOURS BAKING, PLUS COOLING

125g butter, softened, plus extra
 for greasing
250ml milk
1 tbsp white wine vinegar
125g plain chocolate
 (at least 50% cocoa solids),
 broken up
350g self-raising flour, sifted
15g cocoa powder, sifted
1 tsp bicarbonate of soda
250g golden caster sugar
2 medium eggs, beaten

For filling and decoration
4 tbsp sweet sherry or Marsala
 (optional)
185g plain chocolate (at least
 50% cocoa solids), broken up
100g butter, diced
100ml double cream
1 large unsprayed pink rose,
 to decorate

1. Preheat the oven to 160°C/fan 140°C/gas 3. Grease and base-line a deep 20cm-round cake tin with baking paper. Put the milk in a jug and add the vinegar – it will curdle. Melt the chocolate in a large bowl set over a pan of simmering water, making sure the bottom of the bowl doesn't touch the water. Stir until smooth.

2. Add the butter and remaining cake ingredients plus the milk mixture to the chocolate. Beat until smooth, then tip into the tin. Bake for 1¼–1½ hours or until a skewer inserted into the centre comes out clean. Cool in the tin for 10 minutes, then turn out on to a wire rack and cool completely.

3. Cut the cake in half horizontally. Sprinkle the cut sides with sherry or Marsala, if using.

4. Melt the chocolate and butter in a pan over a low heat. Stir until smooth, then remove from the heat. Cool for a few minutes, then beat in the cream. Set aside to thicken slightly.

5. To decorate, use a quarter of the icing to sandwich the 2 cake halves together. Spread the remaining icing over the top and sides of the cake. Decorate with rose petals to serve.

Variation Fill and top the cake with whipped cream or buttercream (see page 182) instead and decorate it with sugar-coated chocolate eggs, chocolate truffles, chocolate shavings, chocolate buttons or curls.

Easter biscuits

Unexpected guests? Want to keep the kids occupied? Make these simple lemony treats from what's in your storecupboard.

MAKES ABOUT 20 BISCUITS
TAKES 25 MINUTES, 15–18 MINUTES
BAKING, PLUS COOLING

150g butter, softened
125g caster sugar, plus extra
  for sprinkling
Finely grated zest of 1 lemon
2 medium egg yolks
250g plain flour, plus extra
  for dusting
½ tsp ground mixed spice
40g currants
10g chopped mixed citrus peel

1. Preheat the oven to 180°C/fan 160°C/gas 4. In a large bowl, beat the butter, sugar and lemon zest until creamy. Beat in the egg yolks until smooth, then beat in the remaining ingredients until the mixture forms a ball.

2. Turn the dough out on to a lightly floured work surface and roll out to about 5mm thickness. Using a 7cm fluted pastry cutter, cut out about 20 biscuits. Re-roll the trimmings as you go. Place on 2 large non-stick baking sheets, spaced a little apart.

3. Bake for 15–18 minutes, until pale golden. Sprinkle with caster sugar, then cool on a wire rack. As a finishing touch, stack a few biscuits and tie with ribbon. They will keep for a week in an airtight container.

Hot cross buns

Everyone loves hot cross buns, so try making your own for an extra-special Easter.

MAKES 12 BUNS
TAKES 45 MINUTES, 15 MINUTES BAKING, PLUS PROVING AND COOLING

625g strong white bread flour
45g chilled butter, plus extra
 for greasing
45g golden caster sugar,
 plus 2 tbsp
1 tsp ground cinnamon
¼ tsp ground allspice
¼ tsp freshly grated nutmeg
1½ tsp fast-action dried yeast
1 egg
275ml milk, plus 4 tbsp
100g raisins
25g chopped mixed peel
Oil, for greasing

Variation To make these even more special, place a small ball of almond paste inside each ball of dough before baking.

1. Sift 500g of the flour into a large bowl. Cut up the butter and rub in with your fingertips until it resembles breadcrumbs. Stir in 45g caster sugar, 1 teaspoon salt, cinnamon, allspice, nutmeg and yeast. Beat the egg in a bowl, then mix it into the dry ingredients with 275ml milk, until you have a soft, pliable dough. Tip the dough out on to a lightly floured surface and knead for 5 minutes, until smooth and elastic. Gradually work in the raisins and peel. Return to the bowl and cover loosely with oiled cling film. Leave in a warm place for 1 hour, until doubled in size (known as proving or rising).

2. Tip the dough out on to a lightly floured surface and knead well to knock out all the air, then cut into 12 pieces. Put your lightly floured hand – slightly cupped, with fingers open – over 1 piece, then rotate your hand in a circular motion, pressing down on the dough to create a neat ball. Repeat with the rest of the dough. Put on 2 greased trays, spaced apart. Cover with oiled cling film and leave in a warm place to rise for 30 minutes.

3. Preheat the oven to 200°C/fan 180°C/gas 6. Sift the remaining flour into a bowl and stir in 125ml water to make a smooth, wet paste. Spoon into a freezer bag, snip off the corner and pipe a cross over each bun. Bake for 15 minutes until golden.

4. Meanwhile, put the extra milk and sugar into a pan. Heat gently to dissolve the sugar, then boil for 2–3 minutes until syrupy. Brush the glaze over the warm buns. Transfer to a wire rack to cool. Serve split open and toasted with lots of butter.

Chocolate and hazelnut panettone

A great alternative to a traditional Christmas cake.

SERVES 12

TAKES 40 MINUTES, 30–35 MINUTES BAKING, PLUS PROVING AND COOLING

125g butter, softened, plus extra for greasing
350g strong white bread flour, plus extra for dusting
7g sachet fast-action dried yeast
50g golden caster sugar
50g raisins
50g roasted hazelnuts, roughly chopped
Finely grated zest of 1 orange
3 large eggs, lightly beaten
4 tbsp warm milk, plus extra, if needed
50g plain chocolate, roughly chopped
Icing sugar, to dust

1. Grease and line a fluted savarin or kugelhopf tin (or a 18cm round x 9cm deep tin). Sift the flour and ½ teaspoon salt into a large bowl. Stir in the yeast, sugar, raisins, nuts and zest.

2. Make a well in the centre and add the eggs, 100g butter and the milk. Mix. Knead in the bowl for 5 minutes or until it is smooth and elastic (add a little extra milk if it's dry).

3. Turn out on to a floured surface and knead for a further 5 minutes or until smooth. Put in a lightly greased bowl and cover with cling film. Leave in a warm place for at least 1 hour or until it has doubled in size (this is known as proving or rising).

4. Punch the dough in the bowl to 'knock back', then knead for another 5 minutes on the floured surface. Gradually knead in the chocolate as quickly as possible to avoid the chunks melting. Shape the dough into a ball and pop into the tin. Cover and leave for another 30 minutes or until risen again.

5. Meanwhile, preheat the oven to 180°C/fan 160°C/gas 4. Melt the remaining 25g butter and brush over the top of the loaf. Bake for 30–35 minutes or until risen. Cool in the tin for 5 minutes, turn out and wrap in a thick tea towel and set aside. Dust with icing sugar to serve.

Sour cherry and marzipan stollen

Marzipan lovers will adore this rich bread surrounding a seam of unadulterated almond paste. To add flavour and crunch, we've used dried sour cherries and plenty of chopped almonds.

SERVES 8–10
TAKES 35 MINUTES, 50 MINUTES BAKING, PLUS PROVING AND COOLING

100g butter, softened, plus extra for greasing
300g strong white bread flour, plus extra for dusting
50g golden caster sugar
7g sachet fast-action dried yeast
Grated zest of 1 orange
100g dried sour cherries
75g whole unblanched almonds, roughly chopped
150ml milk, warmed
125g good-quality marzipan

For the icing
100g icing sugar
3–4 tbsp fresh orange juice

1. Grease a large baking sheet. Sift the flour and ¼ teaspoon salt into a large bowl. Rub in the butter until it resembles fine breadcrumbs. Stir in the sugar, yeast, orange zest, cherries and nuts. Make a well in the centre and gradually pour in the milk. Mix to a soft dough.

2. Turn out on to a floured surface and knead for 10 minutes or until the dough is shiny and elastic. Put the dough into a lightly oiled bowl and cover with cling film. Leave in a warm place for about 1 hour or until it has at least doubled in size (this is known as proving or rising).

3. Punch the dough in the bowl to 'knock back'. Turn out on to a lightly floured surface and roll out to a large rectangle about 20cm x 10cm.

4. Roll the marzipan into a long sausage shape, a little bit shorter than the dough, and lay it down towards the edge of 1 long side of the dough. Fold the dough over so the marzipan is in the centre and press together to seal. Lift on to the baking sheet and cover with lightly greased cling film. Leave to rise for another 30 minutes.

5. Meanwhile, preheat the oven to 160°C/fan 140°C/ gas 3. Bake for about 50 minutes, or until the stollen is golden and sounds hollow when you tap the bottom. Wrap in a thick tea towel and leave to cool. Mix the icing sugar and orange juice together to make a runny icing, spread over the stollen and allow to set. Slice to serve.

Jewelled fruit loaf

A wonderfully fruity loaf that's perfect for a gift or to eat
with the family.

SERVES **8–10**

TAKES **30** MINUTES, **1½–1¾** HOURS
BAKING, PLUS COOLING

Butter, for greasing
100g whole hazelnuts
125g whole almonds
125g stoned dates
150g glacé pineapple
**150g green and red glacé
   cherries**
**150g ready-to-eat dried
   apricots**
150g seedless raisins
100g golden sultanas
Finely grated zest of 1 lemon
100g plain flour
**½ tsp each baking powder,
   ground mixed spice and salt**
125g golden caster sugar
3 large eggs
1 tsp vanilla extract
2 tbsp brandy

1. Preheat the oven to 150°C/fan 130°C/gas 2.
Grease and base-line a 27cm x 11cm loaf tin with
non-stick baking paper. Put the nuts, fruits and zest
into a large bowl. Sift the flour, baking powder, spice
and salt over the fruit. Add the sugar and mix well.

2. Beat together the eggs, vanilla and brandy, then
stir into the mixture. Spoon into the tin and bake
for 1½–1¾ hours, until a skewer inserted into the
middle comes out clean. Leave to cool completely.

3. To assemble your gift, wrap in waxed paper or
clear cellophane and tie with a bow. Keeps in an
airtight box for up to 3 weeks.

Walnut and whisky Christmas cake

A good Christmas cake will last you the whole of the holidays. A great one, like this wonderful walnut and whisky cake, will be around for a couple of days, tops.

SERVES **16**

TAKES ABOUT **25** MINUTES, ABOUT
2½ HOURS BAKING, PLUS COOLING AND
24 HOURS SOAKING

175g raisins
175g sultanas
175g stoned dates, chopped
150g natural glacé cherries,
  halved
100g dried pears, chopped
75g crystallised stem ginger,
  finely chopped
Finely grated zest of 1 lemon
250ml whisky
175g unsalted butter, softened,
  plus extra for greasing
175g dark muscovado sugar
4 eggs, beaten
200g self-raising flour, sifted
1 tbsp golden syrup
2 tsp ground allspice
150g walnut halves, toasted
Fresh bay leaf sprigs, to decorate
Fresh red berries, to decorate

For the whisky butter icing
450g golden icing sugar
150g unsalted butter, softened
3 tbsp glucose syrup
3–4 tbsp whisky

1. Put the raisins, sultanas, dates, cherries, pears, ginger and lemon zest in a large bowl. Pour over the whisky, cover and leave to soak for 24 hours, stirring occasionally, until the fruit has absorbed the liquid.

2. Grease the base and sides of a deep 20cm-round springform cake tin and line with a double thickness of baking paper, ensuring the paper sits higher than the tin. Weigh out 300g of the soaked fruit and tip into a food processor. Blend to a thick, dark purée.

3. Preheat the oven to 150°C/fan 130°C/gas 2. Using an electric hand whisk, beat the butter and sugar together until light and fluffy. Gradually beat in the eggs, adding a little flour to prevent the mixture curdling. Fold in the remaining flour, along with the fruit purée, remaining soaked fruit, the golden syrup, allspice and walnuts, until combined. Spoon into the prepared tin and level the surface. Bake for 2½ hours or until a skewer inserted into the centre of the cake comes out clean. Cool in the tin for 1 hour, turn out and cool completely on a wire rack.

4. Make the whisky butter icing. Gradually beat the icing sugar into the butter, adding the glucose syrup and enough whisky as you go until the icing is smooth and spreadable. Spread over the top and sides of the cake, swirling it with a palette knife. Decorate with the bay leaves and berries to serve.

★ DELICIOUS. TIP Wrap the un-iced cake in baking paper and store in an airtight container in a cool place for up to 3 months. Once iced, store, covered, in the fridge for up to 2 weeks.

Classic Christmas pudding

This show-stopping Christmas pud has everything you could want and more, but the proof, as they say, is in the pudding.

MAKES A 1.5 LITRE PUDDING, SERVES 8
TAKES 30 MINUTES, 5 HOURS STEAMING,
PLUS COOLING AND CHILLING

100g ready-to-eat dried figs, roughly chopped
150g sultanas
150g raisins
150g currants
50g chopped mixed peel
1 Bramley apple, peeled, cored and coarsely grated
Finely grated zest of 1 lemon
50ml Guinness
50ml brandy
150g self-raising flour
2 tsp ground mixed spice
1 tsp freshly grated nutmeg
175g unsalted butter, plus extra for greasing
150g fresh white breadcrumbs
3 medium eggs, lightly beaten
100g molasses sugar
Sprig of holly, to decorate

1. Put the dried fruits, peel, apple, lemon zest, Guinness and brandy into a large bowl, and mix together. In a separate bowl, sieve together the flour, spices and a pinch of salt.

2. Melt the butter in a small pan, then allow to cool slightly. Pour over the dried fruit mixture, then add the breadcrumbs, eggs, molasses sugar and spiced flour. Mix well.

3. Grease and base-line a 1.5 litre pudding basin. Tip in the pudding mixture and level the surface. Cut a circle of foil larger than the top of the pudding basin and make a pleat down the centre. Use to cover the pudding and secure in place with string – tie this around the basin rim, loop over the pudding and tie at the other side to make a handle.

4. Put an upturned saucer in the base of a deep saucepan. Sit the basin on top and fill the pan with boiling water to come halfway up the basin. Cover the pan, bring to the boil, then reduce the heat slightly and steam the pudding for 5 hours, keeping the water level topped up. Using the tie-handle, carefully remove the basin from the saucepan. Set aside to cool. Cover with clean foil and store in a cool place for up to 6 months.

5. To reheat, place on an upturned saucer in a large saucepan of simmering water. Cook for 1 hour or until piping hot throughout.

6. To serve, carefully remove the pudding basin from the pan, uncover the pudding and run a small, sharp knife around it to loosen. Upturn on to a serving plate and decorate with a sprig of holly.

Classic chocolate roulade

Crowd-pleasing, indulgent and easy to make, roulades may be retro but they'll never go out of fashion.

SERVES 6–8
TAKES 50 MINUTES, 12–14 MINUTES BAKING, PLUS COOLING AND SETTING

5 eggs
100g caster sugar, plus extra
  to sprinkle
60g plain flour
40g cocoa powder
1 tsp vanilla extract
1 tsp chocolate extract (optional)

For the ganache and decoration
200g fresh or frozen cranberries
75g caster sugar
400g plain chocolate, broken
  up, plus 200g for leaves,
  to decorate
20g butter, softened
568ml carton double cream
1 tbsp bourbon whiskey
A few holly or bay leaves,
  to decorate
Icing sugar, to dust

1. Preheat the oven to 180°C/fan 160°C/gas 4. Line a Swiss-roll tin with baking paper. Beat the eggs and sugar together with an electric whisk for 5 minutes until thick.

2. Sift over the flour and cocoa, and fold in with the vanilla and chocolate extract, if using. Spread in the tin. Bake for 12–14 minutes. Turn out on to a sheet of baking paper sprinkled with sugar. Cool a little, then roll up from the long side with the paper. Cool on a wire rack.

3. Put the berries, sugar and 2 tablespoons water in a pan and cook for 7–10 minutes. Cool.

4. Put the chocolate and butter in a mixing bowl. Heat 450ml cream in a pan until almost boiling, then pour over the chocolate. Leave for 5 minutes, add the bourbon and stir until smooth. Cool for 10 minutes, then whip until light. Transfer a third of the ganache to a bowl. Whisk in the remaining cream. Unroll the sponge, spread with the creamy ganache, spoon over the cranberries and re-roll.

5. Make the chocoate leaves. Melt the 200g plain chocolate in a heatproof bowl set over a saucepan of simmering water. Leave for 2 minutes, then stir until smooth. Use a clean paint brush to spread a thin layer of chocolate on the underside of clean holly or bay leaves. Allow to set before applying the next coat. Place in the fridge. When set, carefully peel away the leaves to reveal chocolate leaves.

6. Ice the roulade with the remaining ganache. Decorate with the leaves and dust with icing sugar.

Snowflake carrot cupcakes

Get into the spirit of Christmas by making these pretty carrot cupcakes.

MAKES 28 CUPCAKES
TAKES 1½ HOURS, ABOUT 50 MINUTES
BAKING, PLUS COOLING AND SETTING

250ml vegetable oil

3 large carrots (about 350g), grated

75g macadamia nuts, chopped

75g pecan halves, chopped

170g mixed dried berries and cherries

100g ready-to-eat dried figs apricots or prunes, roughly chopped

300g golden granulated sugar

300g self-raising flour

1 tsp ground mixed spice

1 tsp freshly grated nutmeg

2 tsp baking powder

4 large organic eggs

1 quantity chocolate frosting (see page 182)

1 quantity buttercream (see page 182)

500g white sugar paste, Christmas red paste colour, 2 x 2.5g pots clear edible glitter flakes, to decorate

Icing sugar, for dusting

1. Preheat the oven to 180°C/fan 160°C/gas 4. Line 2 x 12-hole muffin tins with muffin cases – you'll need to bake the final 4 later.

2. In a large bowl, combine the oil, carrots, nuts, dried fruit and sugar. Sift over the flour, spices and baking powder and mix thoroughly. Add the eggs, one at a time, and mix until well combined.

3. Divide most of the mixture among the cases, to three-quarters full. Bake for 22–25 minutes, until risen and golden. Repeat with the remaining mixture to make 4 more. Remove from the tin, cool on a wire rack.

4. Pour chocolate frosting over half the cakes – leave to set. Spread the other cakes with buttercream.

5. For the snowflakes, colour half the white sugar paste with the red colouring until it is a deep, rich red – knead until evenly coloured. Roll out to 3mm thick on a surface dusted with icing sugar. Using cutters, cut out a variety of snowflakes and place on a baking sheet lined with baking paper. Repeat with the remaining sugar paste. You need 28 snowflakes in each colour. Set aside to dry and firm up.

6. Brush the snowflakes lightly with water. Sprinkle with edible glitter and arrange on top of the cakes.

Variation Make 1 large cake in a deep 20cm-round loose-bottomed cake tin. Bake for 2–2½ hours, until a skewer inserted into the centre comes out clean. Cover with foil after 1½ hours.

Mince pies

Rich, deep and totally traditional. If you want to make your own mincemeat, try our recipe on page 186.

MAKES 12 DEEP MINCE PIES
TAKES 25 MINUTES, ABOUT
25 MINUTES BAKING, PLUS CHILLING
AND COOLING

350g plain flour, plus extra
  for dusting
175g unsalted butter,
  chilled and cubed
500g jar mincemeat
1 egg, lightly beaten
Icing sugar, to dust

1. Make the pastry. Put the flour, butter and a pinch of salt into a food processor and whiz until the mixture resembles breadcrumbs. Add 3–4 tablespoons cold water and whiz again until the mixture comes together. Tip out on to a lightly floured surface, make a ball and knead lightly until smooth. Wrap in cling film and chill for 30 minutes.

2. Preheat the oven to 190°C/fan 170°C/ gas 5. Cut the pastry into 2 unequal pieces – about two-thirds to one-third. On a lightly floured surface, roll out the larger piece of pastry to about 3mm thick. Using a 10cm-round plain cutter (or ramekin), stamp or cut out 12 circles, re-rolling the trimmings if necessary. Carefully mould into a greased deep 12-hole muffin tin (don't worry if the pastry bunches together, simply smooth out with your fingers). Divide the mincemeat among the pastry cases, filling each one three-quarters full.

3. Roll out the smaller piece of pastry as before and use a 7–8cm-round plain cutter to stamp out 12 lids. Brush the edges of the pastry bases with water, lay a pastry lid on top and press the edges together to seal. Brush each pie with egg. Bake for 25 minutes or until golden and piping hot. Cool in the tin for 5 minutes, then carefully transfer to a wire rack.

4. Serve the mince pies warm or at room temperature, dusted with icing sugar. To store, cool the pies and keep in an airtight container in a cool place for up to 5 days.

Moist, dark fruit Christmas cake

Soaking prunes and dried fruit overnight makes a rich, fruity and ultra-moist Christmas cake that the whole family will love.

GIVES 16 GOOD SLICES
NEEDS OVERNIGHT SOAKING AND TAKES
A LAZY AFTERNOON TO MAKE

175g raisins

175g sultanas

175g ready-to-eat prunes, roughly chopped

150g natural glacé cherries, halved

50g dried blueberries

50g dried cranberries

50g crystallised stem ginger

Grated zest of 1 large orange

250ml brandy (or use whisky or Madeira)

175g unsalted butter, softened

175g dark muscovado sugar

4 eggs, beaten

200g self-raising flour

1 tbsp golden syrup

1 tbsp vanilla extract

1 quantity brandy butter icing (see page 183)

Caramel stars (see page 185), to decorate

1 Put the raisins, sultanas, prunes, cherries, blueberries, cranberries, ginger and orange zest into a large bowl. Pour over the brandy, cover and leave to soak for at least 24 hours, stirring occasionally until most of the brandy has been absorbed.

2. Grease the base and sides of a deep 20cm-round cake tin and line with greaseproof paper.

3. Using a slotted spoon, drain and weigh out 450g of the soaked fruit and put into a food processor. Blend to a thick, dark purée.

4. Preheat the oven to 150°C/fan 130°C/gas 2. In a clean bowl, beat the butter and sugar until light and fluffy. Beat in the eggs a little at a time, adding a little of the flour if it starts to curdle. Add the fruit purée, remaining soaked fruit and brandy, golden syrup, vanilla and remaining flour. Fold everything together until well combined.

5. Spoon into the prepared tin and smooth with the back of the spoon. Bake for 2½–3 hours or until a skewer inserted into the centre comes out clean. Cool in the tin for a few hours, then turn out and cool completely on a wire rack.

6. Swirl the brandy butter icing over the top of the cake, then tie a wide ribbon and bow around the side of the cake. Decorate with the caramel stars. Store in an airtight container and keep in a cool place or the fridge. Eat within 2 weeks.

Boxing Day fridge cake

Savour the memory of Christmas with these delightful chilled treats.

MAKES 16–20 SQUARES
TAKES 10 MINUTES, PLUS CHILLING

500g plain chocolate
100g unsalted butter, plus
  extra for greasing
250g leftover Christmas cake or
  rich fruit cake, chopped
200g Christmas biscuits
  (such as biscotti, amaretti,
  lebkuchen or florentines),
  roughly broken
150g leftover nuts, nougat or
  seasonal dried fruit

1. Melt the plain chocolate with the butter in a bowl set over a pan of barely simmering water.

2. Once melted, stir in the Christmas cake and biscuits and the leftover nuts, nougat or seasonal dried fruit, chopped if large.

3. Spoon into a greased and lined, 20cm-square brownie tin. Chill in the fridge until set, then cut into squares and serve.

Variation Instead of Christmas cake, use a mixture of dried fruits such as raisins, glacé cherries, chopped dried apricots and nuts such as brazil nuts or hazelnuts. You can use digestive biscuits when it's not the Christmas season.

Tips and recipes

Buttercream

Use this recipe to fill or top sponge cakes, cupcakes and muffins, and flavour as desired.

MAKES ENOUGH TO TOP AND FILL
1 LARGE CAKE AND 16 CUPCAKES

125g salted butter, at room
  temperature
250g icing sugar, sifted
1 tsp vanilla extract/grated
  zest 1 orange or lemon/1 tsp
  espresso coffee powder or
  1 tbsp cocoa powder (dissolved
  in 1 tbsp boiling water),
  to flavour

1. Beat the butter and icing sugar together with 1 tablespoon boiling water and your chosen flavouring until smooth and creamy. Cover the surface with cling film and chill until ready to use.

Chocolate frosting

A delicious rich icing for cupcakes and sponge cakes.

MAKES ENOUGH TO TOP AND FILL
1 LARGE CAKE AND 16 CUPCAKES

200g plain chocolate,
  roughly chopped
4 tbsp milk
100g unsalted butter
150g icing sugar

1. Put the chocolate, milk and butter in a small saucepan, and heat gently until the chocolate and butter have melted. Take off the heat and stir into a bowl with the icing sugar until smooth. Cover the surface with cling film and chill until ready to use.

Chocolate ganache

A delicious cream-based chocolate icing for gateaux and rich cakes.

MAKES ENOUGH TO TOP AND FILL
1 LARGE CAKE AND 16 CUPCAKES

350g plain chocolate (at least
  50% cocoa solids), broken up
225ml double cream

1. Melt the chocolate in a large bowl over a pan of gently simmering water, not letting the bottom of it touch the water. Remove from the heat and stir in the cream until smooth. Set aside until thick enough to spread, stirring occasionally.

Cream cheese icing

Use this icing for either carrot cakes and muffins or rich, moist vegetable-based cakes.

MAKES ENOUGH TO TOP AND FILL
1 LARGE CAKE AND 16 CUPCAKES

300g low-fat cream cheese
50g icing sugar, sifted
1 tsp vanilla extract

1. Beat the cream cheese and icing sugar together until smooth and stir in the vanilla extract. Chill until ready to use.

Brandy butter icing

This is a fabulous alternative to royal icing for a Christmas cake.

MAKES ENOUGH TO COVER A 20–23CM
FRUIT CAKE

450g golden icing sugar, sifted
3 tbsp glucose syrup
50g unsalted butter, softened
4 tbsp brandy

1. Put the icing sugar, glucose syrup, butter and brandy into a large bowl and beat until soft and smooth. Swirl over the top of the cake and allow to set a little before adding any decorations.

Royal icing

Use this icing to top Christmas cakes or for piping decoration.

MAKES ENOUGH TO COVER A 20–23CM
FRUIT CAKE

3 medium egg whites
Juice of ½ lemon
800g icing sugar, sifted
**Food colouring (your choice of
  colours)**

1. Put the egg whites, lemon juice and half the icing sugar in a bowl and stir until smooth. Gradually stir in the rest of the icing sugar until the mixture is smooth and forms soft peaks. Cover the icing with cling film or place in a sealed plastic bowl to prevent it drying out until ready to use.

2. Add food colourings as desired.

Rich shortcrust pastry

This is the ideal rich, crumbly pastry for making mince pies and tarts. Make, then wrap in cling film for 10 minutes before using.

170g plain flour
Pinch of salt
**100g cold unsalted butter,
  cut into cubes**
1 tbsp caster sugar
1 large egg yolk

1. Sift the flour and salt into a mixing bowl. Add the butter, then rub between fingertips until the mixture resembles breadcrumbs.

2. Sift in the caster sugar, then add the egg yolk and mix quickly with a palette knife. Add 2–4 tablespoons cold water, mixing with the knife until the mixture is drawn together into a dough. Press into a ball. Cover with cling film and chill for at least 10 minutes.

Caramel stars

Here's a simple but effective decoration that looks great on both cakes and desserts.

225g granulated sugar
Oil, for greasing

1. Put the sugar into a small heavy-based saucepan and dissolve very slowly over a gentle heat. Continue cooking without stirring until it begins to turn a pale caramel colour. Remove from the heat and slowly drizzle a little of the caramel on to a lightly oiled baking sheet in the shape of a star (if you find it easier, use a spoon to drizzle the caramel). If the caramel begins to set in the pan, return to the heat to dissolve again. Leave until set.

Tips for making the perfect roulade

A classic chocolate roulade is a brilliant dessert for dinner parties because you can assemble the roulade up to 5 hours ahead, it cooks in no time at all.

★ When you line the Swiss-roll tin with a sheet of non-stick baking paper, trim the paper to stand proud of the tin by 3cm. This will give the roulade space to rise.

★ For best results use an electric hand whisk or mixer to whisk the eggs and sugar together at top speed until thick, pale and airy – the beaters should leave a ribbon-like trail behind when lifted.

★ Use eggs that are a few days old and bring them up to room temperature before whisking – they will whip up more easily and make the roulade lighter.

★ When folding the flour and cocoa powder into the whisked egg mixture, try to retain as much air as possible, in order to keep the sponge light. Use a large metal spoon or a spatula and gently cut through the mixture, rotating the bowl as you do so.

Mincemeat

Use this recipe if you want to make your own mincemeat for our mince pies and streusel recipes.

MAKES ABOUT 1.1KG MINCEMEAT
TAKES 50 MINUTES, PLUS COOLING AND
STERILISING JARS

1 large Bramley apple, peeled,
  cored and coarsely grated
100g sultanas
75g currants
75g dried cranberries
175g raisins
100g mixed chopped peel
25g pecan nuts, finely chopped
100ml dark rum
Finely grated zest of 1 orange,
  plus the juice of 2
Finely grated zest and juice
  of 1 lemon
2 tsp ground mixed spice
½ tsp ground cloves
½ tsp ground ginger
½ tsp freshly grated nutmeg
175g dark muscovado sugar
100g shredded vegetable suet

1. Combine all the ingredients except the muscovado sugar and suet in a large saucepan. Place over a low heat and cook, stirring occasionally, for 30 minutes or until the fruit has plumped up and most of the liquid has evaporated, don't let it become dry. Set aside to cool, then stir in the muscovado sugar and suet.

2. Meanwhile, sterilise several jars. Preheat the oven to 120°C/fan 100°C/gas ½. Wash both the jars and lids well in hot, soapy water, rinse and place upside down on a baking sheet. Place in the hot oven for 10 minutes or until dry. Remove from the oven and use a clean cloth to handle the jars.

3. Divide the mincemeat among the hot jars, seal, label and set aside to cool.

★ DELICIOUS. TIP You can store the mincemeat in a sterilised jar in a cool place for up to 6 months.

How to line a round cake tin

Cut out 1 circle of baking paper to fit the base of the tin, and 1 long length about 4cm taller than the tin. Snip short cuts along the long edge, and fit it inside the tin with the snipped cuts resting on the base. Sit the circle of paper on top.

How to line a square cake tin

Cut and snip in the same way as for a round tin, but cut 4 lengths of paper for the sides and a square piece for the base.

How to line a Swiss-roll tin

Line the tin with a sheet of non-stick baking paper, trim the paper to stand proud of the tin by 3cm. Snip into the corners of the paper so that it fits tightly into the tin.

How to make a piping bag

Cut 2 pieces of greaseproof paper into 25cm squares, then cut each piece diagonally into 2. In your left hand, hold the middle of the long side of 1 triangle (it'll look like an arrow pointing right). Make a cone by rolling the top corner with your right hand to meet the right-angle of the triangle, and hold with your thumb and forefinger. Using your left hand, roll the final corner around to meet the other 2. Fold the tips of the 3 corners inside the cone. Repeat with the other 3 triangles and set aside.

Cake-decorating suppliers

Here's a list of useful suppliers for all your cake-baking and decorating needs.

For sugar paste, edible food colourings, fondant icings, cake boards and all specialist cake-decorating supplies go to www.squires-shop.com

Buy cake colours, edible lustre powder, nylon piping bags and nozzles from www.rainbowsugarcraft.co.uk.

Novelty cake tins www.the partycakeshop.co.uk

Snowflake cutters are available from good cook shops or from www.coxandcox.co.uk

For a good selection of biscuit cutters, visit www.cakecraftshop.co.uk

General bakeware and a good selection of cake tins, visit www.lakeland.co.uk

For a great range of aluminium bakeware and cake tins, including a square cake tin with dividers so you can make mini square cakes, or mini round cake tins, try www.alansilverwood.co.uk

www.splatcooking.net for cookie cutters, cake cases, aprons, glitters, sprinkles, cake stands, gingerbread and other cooking stuff

Index

almonds 164
  cake in spiced citrus syrup
    72–3
  and orange and chocolate
    dessert cake 88–9
  paste 154, 160, 164
  Richmond maids of honour
    56–7
apples
  and oats and cinnamon
    cookies 108–9
  and pecan and raisin
    muffins 24–5
apricots 12, 36, 108, 180
  buttermilk cake 60–1
Archer, Val 24

bacon 146
bananas 24
bars
  black cherry and pistachio
    cereal 38–9
  power 18–19
basil and goat's cheese
    cornbread 138–9
beetroot chocolate cake 90–1
biscuits 104–19
  digestive 180
  Easter 158–9
blueberries 96, 142
Boxing Day fridge cake 180–1
brandy butter icing 178, 183
bread 120–33, 136–7
  cherry and pecan plait
    124–5
  Cornish saffron festival loaf
    136–7
  feta, tomato and rosemary
    flowerpot 128–9
  milk 132–3

white rustic loaf 122–3
brownies, chocolate chunk
    102–3
buns 136
  Chelsea,
cardamom-scented
    134–5
  hot cross 160–1; biggest
    152–3
butter cream 156, 182
  chocolate 84
  coffee 78, 84
  peanut 114
  praline 94
  vanilla 46, 182
butterfly cakes 46
buttermilk apricot cake 60–1

cakes, classic 44–85; small
    10–43
caramel stars 178, 185
cardamom-scented Chelsea
    buns 134–5
carrot
  cake 76–7
  and coriander muffins
    142–3
  snowflake cupcakes 174–5
cheese 142
  Cheshire 54
  and ham and mustard
    muffins 144–5
  and mustard scones 146–7
cherries 12, 40, 96, 180
  black and pistachio cereal
    bars 38–9
  and pecan plait 124–5
  sour and marzipan stollen
    164–5
chocolate 24, 86–103

beetroot cake 90–1
  butter cream 84
  chip cookies 110–11
  chunk brownies 102–3
  cranberry muffins 12–13
  double chocolate toffee
    cookies 112–13
  frosting 182
  fruity flapjacks 96–7
  ganache 88, 92, 100, 172,
    183
  and hazelnut pannetone
    162–3
  and hazelnut truffles 100–1
  meringues 40–1
  and orange and almond
    dessert cake 88–9
  peanut crumble cookies
    116–17
  praline fancies 94–5
  rose-petal cake 156–7
  roulade, classic 172–3, 185
  rum and raisin torte 92–3
  toffee crispy cakes 30–1
Christmas baking 162–81
Christmas cake 178–9
  walnut and whisky 168–9
Christmas pudding, classic
    170–1
cinnamon and oats and apple
  cookies 108–9
citrus syrup, spiced, almond
  cake in 72–3
coconut slice 14–15
  and lime slice 16–17
coffee 42
  butter cream 78, 84
  and mascarpone liqueur 84
  and pecan roulade 84–5
  and walnut cake with

tiramisu cream 78–9
conversion tables 8–9
cookies
    chocolate chip 110–11
    chocolate peanut crumble
        116–17
    double chocolate toffee
        112–13
    oat, apple and cinnamon
        108–9
    peanut butter and cranberry
        114–15
    snowball 118–19
coriander and carrot muffins
    142–3
cornbread, basil and goat's
    cheese 138–9
cornflakes 30
Cornish saffron festival loaf
    136–7
courgette muffins/cake 26–7
cranberries 96
    chocolate muffins 12–13
    fruit loaf with cranberry
        sauce 64–5
    and peanut butter cookies
        114–15
cream 156
    maple syrup 106
    tiramisu with coffee and
        walnut cake 78–9
cream cheese frosting/icing
    76, 183
    with poppy seed and lemon
        cake 80–1
    with spiced pumpkin
        muffins 28–9
crème fraîche 88
crème patissière with Vanilla
    sponge and gooseberry

compote 58–9
crispy cakes, chocolate toffee
    30–1
cupcakes, carrot snowflake
    174–5

dates
    crumb cake 36–7
    puréed 20
    and walnuts and granola
        and honey cake 82–3
decorations 28, 84, 88, 92, 154,
    156, 166, 172, 174, 178
    suppliers 187
drizzle
    lemon 66
    orange 74
Dundee cake 50–1

Easter baking 152–61
Easter biscuits 158–9
Eccles cakes 54–5
elderflower syrup with
    gooseberry streusel cake
    22–3

fancies 94
    chocolate praline 94–5
feta, tomato and rosemary
    flowerpot bread 128–9
flapjacks
    low-sugar, low-fat 20–1
    fruity chocolate 96–7
foccacia, olive and thyme
    130–1
frangipane, iced with
    raspberry tarts 32–3
freezing 114, 116, 140, 142,
    144, 148
frosting

chocolate 182
    cream cheese with spiced
        pumpkin muffins 28–9
fruit loaf
    cranberry with cranberry
        sauce 64–5
    jewelled 166–7
    and parsnip loaf with lemon
        drizzle 66–7
fruits, dried 12, 108, 154, 178,
    180

ginger
    cake, moist 62–3
    loaf cake 68–9
goat's cheese
    and basil cornbread 138–9
    and spinach muffins 140–1
gooseberry
    compote and crème
        patissière with Vanilla
        sponge 58–9
    streusel cake with
        elderflower syrup 22–3
granola and walnuts and
    honey and date cake 82–3
Grigson, Jane 64

ham 142
    and cheese and mustard
        muffins 144–5
hazelnuts 180
    and chocolate pannetone
        162–3
    and chocolate truffles 100–1
    liqueur 94
    and meringue roulade 70–1
honey and walnuts and
    granola and date cake
    82–3

ice cream 102
icing 66, 90, 164
    brandy butter 178, 183
    cream cheese 80, 183
    fondant 94
    royal 184
    whisky butter 168
    yogurt 82

jam 14, 48, 56, 84

leftovers 92, 138, 180
lemon 72
    drizzle with parsnip and
        fruit loaf 66–7
    and poppy seed cake with
        cream cheese frosting
80–1
lime and coconut slice 16–17
lining tins 185, 187
loaf
    Cornish saffron festival
        136–7
    ginger 68–9

maple and raspberry
    shortcakes 106–7
marrons glacées 92
marzipan and sour cherry
    stollen 164–5
mascarpone
    and coffee liqueur 84
    and pesto and tomato
        pastry wheels 148–9
meringues
    chocolate 40–1
    hazelnut roulade 70–1
    mocha 42–3
mince pies 176–7

mincemeat 34, 186
mocha meringues 42–3
muffins
    apple, pecan and raisin
24–5
    carrot and coriander 142–3
    chocolate cranberry 12–13
    courgette 26–7
    ham, cheese and mustard
        144–5
    spiced pumpkin with cream
        cheese frosting 28–9
    spinach and goat's cheese
        140–1
mustard
    and cheese scones 146–7
    and ham and cheese
        muffins 144–5

nougat 180
Nutella 70
nuts 12, 18, 40, 98, 180
nutty tray bake 98–9

oat, apple and cinnamon
    cookies 108–9
olive and thyme foccacia
130–1
orange
    and almond and chocolate
        dessert cake 88–9
    drizzle 74
    fruit salad 72
    juice 164
    and rosemary polenta cake
        74–5

pannetone, chocolate and
    hazelnut 162–3

parkin 52–3
Parmesan 138, 140, 146
parsnip and fruit loaf with
    lemon drizzle 66–7
pastry, shortcrust 32, 34, 184
    wheels, pesto, mascarpone
        and tomato 148–9
peanut
    butter and cranberry
        cookies 114–15
    and chocolate crumble
        cookies 116–17
pecan
    and apple and raisin
        muffins 24–5
    and cherry plait 124–5
    and coffee roulade 84–5
pesto, mascarpone and
    tomato pastry wheels
    148–9
pineapaple 60
piping bag 187
pistachio and black cherry
    cereal bars 38–9
plums 60
polenta cake, orange and
    rosemary 74–5
poppy seed and lemon cake
    with cream cheese
    frosting 80–1
praline fancies, chocolate
94–5
prunes 78
pumpkin
    muffins, spiced with cream
        cheese frosting 28–9
    seeds with brown knot rolls
        126–7

raisins 12, 108, 180
   and apple and pecan
      muffins 24–5
   and rum torte, chocolate
      92–3
raspberry
   jam 84
   maple shortcakes 106–7
   tarts with iced frangipane
      32–3
rhubarb 60
Rice Krispies 30
Richmond maids of honour
   56–7
rolls, brown knot with
   pumpkin seeds 126–7
rose petals
   chocolate cake 156–7
   crystallised 80
rosemary
   and feta and tomato
      flowerpot bread 128–9
   and orange polenta cake
      74–5
roulade 185
   chocolate, classic 172–3,
      185
   coffee and pecan 84–5
   hazelnut meringue 70–1
rum and raisin torte,
   chocolate 92–3

saffron festival loaf, Cornish
   136–7
scones, cheese and mustard
   146–7
seeds 18
   poppy and lemon cake with
      cream cheese frosting
80–1

pumpkin with brown knot
   rolls 126–7

sherry 156
shortcakes, raspberry maple
   106–7
simnel cakes, mini 154–5
snowball cookies 118–19
spice, mixed 12
spinach and goat's cheese
   muffins 140–1
stollen, sour cherry and
   marzipan 164–5
storage 30, 38, 40, 50, 52, 56,
   82,92, 100, 108, 116, 118,
   158, 166, 168, 170, 176,
   178
strawberries 12, 40
   jam 48
streusel 34–5
   gooseberry with elderflower
      syrup 22–3
Swiss roll 84
syrup
   elderflower with gooseberry
      streusel cake 22–3
   maple 106
   spiced citrus, almond cake
      in 72–3

tarts
   raspberry with iced
      frangipane 32–3
   Richmond maids of honour
      56–7
thyme 146
   and olive foccacia 130–1
tips 68, 92, 114, 118, 140, 142,
   144, 148, 168, 176, 185–7
   passim

tiramisu cream with coffe and
   walnut cake 78–9

toffee
   crispy cakes, chocolate
30–1
   and double chocolate
      cookies 112–13
tomato
   and feta and rosemary
      flowerpot bread 128–9
   and pesto and mascarpone
      pastry wheels 148–9
toppings 16, 32
torte, chocolate rum and
   raisin 92–3
truffles, chocolate and
   hazelnut 100–1

vanilla butter cream 46, 182
Vanilla sponge with crème
   patissière and gooseberry
   compote 58–9
Victoria sponge 46–7
   mini 48–9
vinegar, balsamic 130

walnuts
   and coffee cake with
      tiramisu cream 78–9
   and granola and honey and
      date cake 82–3
   and whisky Christmas cake
      168–9
whisky and walnut Christmas
   cake 168–9

yogurt 66
   icing 82

Picture and recipe credits

Harper Collins would like to thank the following for providing photographs:

Steve Baxter p17, p23, p25, p59, p61, p145, p149, p173; Malou Burger p33, p35; Peter Cassidy p75; Tara Fisher p31, p115; Jonathan Gregson p65, p93; Richard Jung p95, p117, pp150–1, p169, p171, p175, p177; Lis Parsons p13, p29, pp44–45, p73, p79, p81, p85; Michael Paul pp10–11, p15, p19, p21, p37, p47, p49, p51, p53, p55, p57, p69, p99, p109, p111, p113, p119, p139, p141, p143, p147, p153, p155, p157, p159, p167, p179;

Claire Richardson p63, p97, p133; Craig Robertson pp86–7, p103; Brett Stevens p100, pp120–1, p135, p137, p163, p165; Lucinda Symons p41, p89, p161; Karen Thomas p27, p67, p77, p91; Kate Whitaker pp104–5, p107; Stuart West p181; Rob White p39, p43, p71, p83, p123, p125, p127, p129, p131

With thanks to the following for creating the recipes for delicious. which are used in this book:

Felicity Barnum-Bobb p62, p132; Kate Belcher p42, p48, p70, p108, p110, p112, p122, p124, p126, p128, p130, p144, p148, p168, p170, p176; Katie Bishop p100, p134, p136, p162, p164; Angela Boggiano p22, p26, p28, p66, p76, p90, p92, p96, p102; Matthew Drennan p16, p88, p118, p160, p166, p178; Silvana Franco p74; Brian Glover p68, p138, p146; Amanda Grant p30, p114; Alice Hart p38, p58, p60, p82, p84, p94, p172; Debbie Major p72, p78, p80, p174; Hannah Miles p106, p116; Tom Norrington-Davies p64; Lizzie Webb-Wilson p32, p34, p180; Mitzie Wilson p12, p14, p18, p20, p24, p36, p40, p46, p50, p52, p54, p56, p98, p140, p142, p152, p154, p156, p158